P O I S O N I N G
THE PECKS
of **GRAND RAPIDS**

POISONING
THE PECKS
of GRAND RAPIDS

THE SCANDALOUS 1916
MURDER PLOT

TOBIN T. BUHK

THE
History
PRESS

Published by The History Press
Charleston, SC 29403
www.historypress.net

Copyright © 2014 by Tobin T. Buhk
All rights reserved

First published 2014

Manufactured in the United States

ISBN 978.1.62619.697.1

Library of Congress CIP data applied for.

CONTENTS

CONTENTS

ACKNOWLEDGEMENTS

The author would like to thank the following for their gracious help and support in locating and acquiring source material: the Library of Congress, the Municipal Archives of New York, the State Archives of New York, the Lloyd Sealy Library at the John Jay College of Criminal Justice, the Loutit District Library (Grand Haven, Michigan) and fellow authors and researchers Amberrose Hammond and Jennifer Richmond.

INTRODUCTION

NEW YORK, NEW YORK

Sunday Morning, March 12, 1916

The groaning grew louder in intensity, jarring Arthur Warren Waite from a deep slumber. The poison was working, just not fast enough. He sat upright on the couch that he had placed outside the bedroom door and eyed the bottle of chloroform. He did not want the sounds to wake his wife, Clara, who was fast asleep in the next room. If she awoke and insisted on calling a doctor, his plot might collapse.

Waite grabbed the bottle and gently opened the door. He cringed as the door creaked on its hinges.

John Peck lay curled into a fetal position. As Waite approached the bedside, Peck opened his eyes slightly. With his sleeve, he wiped away the froth at the corners of his mouth and attempted to sit up, but Waite gently pushed him back into a prone position.

"Here is a little ether and a little aromatic spirits of ammonia mixed," Waite whispered, "and that will quiet you and stop the pain of retching."

"Yes, all right," Peck moaned. "All right."[1]

Waite grinned as he uncorked the bottle and doused John Peck's handkerchief with chloroform. Peck's eyes watered as Waite pressed the rag against his mouth, but after a few minutes, the old man appeared to be unconscious.

Waite tiptoed into the hallway, pulled a pillow off the couch and crept back into the bedroom. He stood over his father-in-law for a few seconds and smiled at the sight of the once formidable plutocrat, now reduced to a pale figure lying helpless in his vomit-encrusted nightclothes. Waite gripped the pillow with both hands, placed it over Peck's face and pushed downward. The corded muscles of his forearms bulged and the backs of his palms turned white as he held the pillow in place. John Peck clawed at the air for a few seconds before his arms dropped to his waist and all movement ceased.[2] Waite lifted Peck's arm, dropped it and watched the lifeless limb fall onto the bed, leaving a dent in the sheet. Then he felt the wrist for a pulse, but there was none.

Waite sat on the edge of the bed, wiped his glistening forehead with the back of his sleeve and took several deep breaths before retreating into the hallway, gently closing the bedroom door on his way. Exhausted, he slumped back onto the couch and decided to rest for a little while before breaking the sad news to Clara that her father had died of natural causes. It would be rough on her. Her mother had passed away in the same room just six weeks before.

He already knew what he would tell Clara; he had scripted his lines weeks ago and had rehearsed them a dozen times since then. He would tell her that the recent loss of her father's lifelong partner was just too much for the old man's frail heart.

Waite giggled as he thought about the moment of truth at the altar of the Fountain Street Baptist Church the previous September when Clara Louise Peck became "Mrs. Waite." As soon as Clara uttered, "I do," she unknowingly set his plot to poison the Pecks in motion.

PART I

TWISTED FAIRY TALE

THE PRINCESS AND THE PAUPER

GRAND RAPIDS, MICHIGAN

Thursday, September 9, 1915

Friends, family and even a few reporters crammed the pews of the Fountain Street Baptist Church to witness the social event of the year. To Grand Rapids high society, the marriage of Arthur Warren Waite to Clara Louise Peck was the last chapter in a fairy-tale romance between a debutante and a debonair suitor from the other side of the tracks.

The son of fruit and vegetable wholesaler Warren Winfield Waite, Arthur grew up in a modestly sized house on the north side of the city. A decade earlier, his parents had moved from Cannonsburg Township to Grand Rapids so their three boys—Clyde, Frank and Arthur—could receive a proper education at Grand Rapids High School.[3] Warren did his best to provide for his family, but money was never plentiful, so Arthur delivered papers for the *Herald* as he attended primary school. In 1905, Arthur—a star athlete, a member of the school's literary society and the all-American boy—graduated from high school and went to the University of Michigan, where he began his study of dentistry.

Clara grew up in a mansion on a hill overlooking the city. Her father, business tycoon John Edward Peck, had come to Grand Rapids forty years earlier and worked his way from a pharmacy proprietor to a wealthy entrepreneur.

The son of New York physician Elias Peck, John learned the pharmacy business by helping his father run his family's drugstore alongside his brother Thomas. In 1865, Thomas Peck briefly left the business. A few years later, John married Hannah Carpenter, and the couple relocated to Grand

Left: An advertising card for Hoyt's German Cologne, circa 1900—one of the many products available from Peck Bros. *From the author's collection.*

Below: Peck Bros. distributed these cards to customers. *From the author's collection.*

HOYT'S GERMAN COLOGNE.

The most Fragrant and Lasting of all Perfumes.

Beware of Counterfeits and Imitations.

We put up no article of Perfumery excepting HOYT'S GERMAN COLOGNE; any other preparation represented as coming from us is an IMPOSITION and a FRAUD. Ask for HOYT'S GERMAN COLOGNE, and before purchasing see that the name is blown in the bottle, the signature of the proprietors printed in red ink across the label, and as an additional guarantee of genuineness observe our PRIVATE United States Revenue Stamp over the cork.

Trial Size, Price 25 cts.;.................Large Bottles, $1.00.

SOLD BY ALL DRUGGISTS AND FANCY GOODS DEALERS.

E. W. HOYT & CO., Proprietors, Lowell, Mass.

FOR SALE BY

PECK BROS., 129 Monroe St., Grand Rapids, Mich.,

DEALERS IN

Drugs, Patent Medicines, Chemicals, Fancy and Toilet Articles, Brushes, Perfumery, &c., &c.

Grand Rapids Chair Company, circa 1905–1920. John and Thomas Peck—founders of Peck Bros.—opened for business in 1875, just about the time Grand Rapids began to evolve into a metropolis. Over the next few decades, it would become the nation's Furniture City, and John Peck would become one of the city's most influential businessmen. *From the Detroit Publishing Company, Library of Congress.*

Monroe Street scene, Grand Rapids, circa 1900–1910. As a successful entrepreneur, John E. Peck's business activities ranged from investor to executive, culminating in holdings worth seven figures in 1916. Among his many roles, he served as president of the National City Bank, seen here at the far left. *From the Detroit Publishing Company, Library of Congress.*

Postcard showing Canal Street in 1914. *From the author's collection.*

Postcard showing Monroe Street in 1914. By this time, Grand Rapids had evolved from a small river town to a bustling metropolis. Peck's drugstore stood at the corner of Division and Monroe, a spot where two of the city's major arteries intersected. *From the author's collection.*

Rapids, Michigan, where John and Thomas opened a drug business that later evolved into Peck Brothers.[4]

Despite keen competition, the Peck enterprise flourished as the lumbering boom transformed Grand Rapids into a metropolis. John's fortune snowballed when he invested in other enterprises. He acquired real estate, served as president of the National City Bank, founded the Alabastine Company and invested in the Widdicomb Furniture Company. By 1916, his portfolio's value eclipsed seven figures.[5]

Clara enjoyed all of the privileges available to a young heiress. She drank tea served in the finest china, and her playmates included the daughters of lumber barons, industrialists and bankers. As a teenager, she left Grand Rapids to attend Chevy Chase Finishing School for young society ladies in Washington, D.C. Following graduation, she attended Columbia University in New York.

Her romance with Waite began with a waltz in 1906, when nineteen-year-old Arthur got up enough nerve to ask sixteen-year-old Clara for a dance. He had just finished his freshman year in college; she was home from finishing school for summer break. Neither partner realized, as they whirled around the parquet floor, that their dance would one day lead to an epic climax at the altar of the Fountain Street Baptist Church.

Over the next few years, Arthur and Clara would occasionally bump into each other at society soirees. Clara found Waite's charm alluring, and she was flattered by the attention of such a handsome man. She felt drawn to him; his drive to succeed reminded her of her father.

Upon graduation, Arthur traveled to Scotland, where he completed a special course for dental surgery before taking a job in South Africa. As an employee of Wellman & Bridgeman—a well-known British dental firm—he made an excellent salary that he invested in real estate, eventually acquiring two farms. This vision of Arthur Warren Waite—the local boy raised on stew but who had earned a seat eating caviar at the society table—was celebrated throughout Grand Rapids as a living, breathing example of the American dream.

Despite being half a world away, Waite never forgot about that dance with Clara Peck. Determined to stay in touch, he sent her a letter. Thrilled to have received a letter from an exotic locale like Durban, Clara responded, which led to an on-again, off-again correspondence.

Then, in late 1914, Clara heard through the society grapevine that Waite had returned from Africa and had established a dental practice in New York City. Curious about his African adventures, she sent him an invitation to a reception her mother was hosting.[6] Waite came knocking on the door of

Dr. Arthur Warren Waite
in 1916. *From the Bain News
Service, Library of Congress.*

the Peck residence with a South African accent, a trove of stories and an infatuation for one of the city's most eligible bachelorettes.

Throughout the winter of 1915, Waite wooed Clara. Reluctant to tie the knot, she didn't say "yes" when Waite first proposed. Undaunted, he followed the Peck family to Miami, where they went to escape the harsh Michigan winter. Eventually, Clara could no longer resist, and she accepted his offer of a diamond ring. They agreed to a September wedding.

———◆———

Reverend Dr. Alfred Wesley Wishart, Bible in hand, stood by the altar next to Arthur. Sunshine flooded through the stained-glass windows, casting white beams across the pews of the sanctuary as ushers struggled to find seats for the stragglers who had arrived just in time to see the nuptials.

Clara Waite's older brother, Percy Peck, circa 1916. *From the Bain News Service, Library of Congress.*

Percy Peck glared at the groom as he waited for the marriage ceremony to begin. Waite was too good to be true, and Percy knew it. He just couldn't convince his sister Clara to dump Waite and instead turn her attention to her childhood sweetheart, John Caulfield. Percy glanced at Caulfield, one of the ushers, and then looked back at Waite, who was standing at the altar waiting for his bride-to-be to make her entrance. His ear-to-ear grin and the smug way he tilted his head back made Percy cringe.

Percy didn't trust the Johnny-come-lately. He knew some of Arthur's classmates at the University of Michigan who described several incidents of theft that ranged from petit larceny to outright fraud.

Waite, apparently, also had a problem keeping his fly closed.

Just a few weeks before the wedding, Waite went to visit Clara's friend Margaret Fisher. While there, he became smitten with Catherine Hubbs, a society deb from Bethlehem, Pennsylvania. Waite tried to sweet-talk Ms. Hubbs out of her dress for a night of torrid lovemaking. Overcome with rapture, he proposed to her, but Hubbs knew of his engagement to Clara.

"You are engaged to Clara Peck," she scolded him. "You have no right to propose to me."

Waite denied everything, so Hubbs whipped off a letter to Grand Rapids. Clara sent a reply, confirming the engagement. Both Fisher and Hubbs responded, pleading with her, "Don't marry him, please."[7] Upon hearing about the letters, Percy joined the chorus trying to dissuade Clara, but she retorted that she would marry Waite if it killed her.

Then, on the eve of the wedding, Percy received an anonymous telegram with an ominous warning: "Don't let Clara marry Arthur Waite. If you do, you will be sorry."[8] When Percy showed the letter to Clara, she gave a slight chuckle. Percy recognized it as the same small laugh she often used when she confronted an uncomfortable question. With degrees in law and pharmacy, Percy was an educated man with a keen insight into human nature, and he saw Waite as a poseur, but Clara seemed blinded by her devotion.[9]

Percy understood how Clara could fall for someone like Waite. As a child, Waite was skinny, gangly and awkward, but years on high school sports teams had transformed him into a trim, athletic specimen. He also had an irresistible charm to go along with the boyish good looks. When he returned to Grand Rapids in 1914, his smile sent shock waves throughout the city's female population. Wherever he went, Arthur Warren Waite enjoyed gangs of swooning admirers.

Percy looked at his mother, Hannah, who was sitting in the front pew. She was another victim of Waite's considerable charm. Hannah Carpenter Peck cherished the time she spent sipping tea with Arthur in the front parlor. Like her, Arthur had an appreciation for language and music, and she delighted in the tales he told of his adventures in Africa. His stories of treating Africa's underprivileged appealed to the strong sense of brotherly love she learned

Hannah Peck, who died mysteriously while visiting the Waites' Coliseum Apartment in January 1916. *From the Bain News Service, Library of Congress.*

as the child of a prominent New York Quaker. It was a legacy she carried to Grand Rapids, where, alongside John, she gave back to the city through several philanthropic endeavors.

Waite knew exactly how to handle the Peck matriarch. Whenever they met, Arthur grasped her hand, holding it for a few seconds and gently caressing her palm with his thumb. It always brought her comfort. John used to do that after they lost their fifteen-year-old daughter, Bessie.[10]

Hannah became Waite's staunchest ally at the Peck residence. She knew that Clara had some doubts about marrying Waite. In the days leading up to the wedding, the Pecks held several family discussions about the match. Percy and John urged Clara to learn more about Waite's past before she said "I do," but Hannah always took Waite's side.

She even referred to Arthur as "my little boy," which chafed Percy. Everyone knew this, of course, so when he complained about the match, they just shrugged it off as petty jealousy.[11] In fact, it was Hannah Peck who pressed for the September marriage. Arthur wanted to wait until the spring, but Mother, in ill health, wanted to see her daughter married before it was too late.[12]

Percy turned sharply when the "Bridal Chorus" filled the sanctuary. He smiled as he watched his little girl, Florence, leading the wedding procession with a basket of pink rose petals in the crook of her arm. Next in the procession was the matron of honor—Percy's wife, Ella—decked out in a white satin gown with Chantilly lace trim.[13]

Clara, hanging on to the arm of her father, followed Ella. The *Grand Rapids News* correspondent described the bride as she slowly stepped toward the altar: "She was handsomely gowned in white duchess satin, trimmed here and there with shimmering silver tones, and made with a court train which fell from the shoulders and was edged with silver lace."[14]

Once the soon-to-be bride and groom were ensconced by the altar, Reverend Wishart began the ceremony. Clara's mind drifted as Wishart read a passage from his Bible. She thought about their first dance in 1906, how he led her across the floor, his eyes never leaving hers, as if she was the only woman in the room. How the warmth of his hand on the small of her back sent a shiver through her, like an electric impulse that touched every part of her body at once.

She thought about the journey Mr. and Mrs. Arthur Warren Waite would make from the altar: a lavish reception at the Peck residence followed by their first night together at the posh Hotel Pontchartrain in Detroit and finally on to a seven-room flat at Manhattan's Coliseum Apartments.

"Do you, Clara Louise Peck…" Wishart's question awakened her from her reverie.

She smiled as she said, "I do." The man whom every woman wanted now belonged to her.

"Do you, Arthur Warren Waite, take…"

The Hotel Pontchartrain in Detroit, where Clara and Arthur spent their first night together. After their stay in Detroit, the newlyweds traveled to New York. They lived in a hotel while their Coliseum Apartment was being prepared. *From the Detroit Publishing Company, Library of Congress.*

Arthur smirked. The Peck family had no idea what he had planned for them. Saying "I do" would set his grand scheme in motion.

Reverend Wishart paused and looked at Arthur Warren Waite.

"I do," he said and grinned.

"K. ADAMS"

NEW YORK, NEW YORK

Monday Morning, March 13, 1916

Waite glared at Clara as the Wolverine Express sped toward Grand Rapids, Michigan. She stared out the window, her hands folded in her lap in a pose that reminded him of a contrite schoolgirl. Her mourning dress made her complexion appear even more pale than usual.

She didn't suspect a thing.

When Hannah came to visit the newlyweds at their Coliseum Apartment on January 10 and fell mysteriously ill, Clara had no idea what really caused her sickness. Even after Hannah suddenly and unexpectedly passed away three weeks later from kidney disease, Clara still didn't question the cause of death scrawled on her mother's death certificate.

Kidney failure—Waite couldn't help but laugh at the thought. He looked away from Clara and giggled.

He even managed to convince the Pecks that Hannah wanted a cremation, and they didn't suspect his ulterior motive of destroying evidence when he took the body to a Detroit crematorium. When he brought Hannah's ashes back to Grand Rapids, where they were interred at Oak Hill Cemetery, the family had no idea that he had just completed the first phase of a malevolent plot.

Then, six weeks later, John Peck traveled to New York. Grieving his wife's untimely passing, he decided to take solace by spending some time with his daughter. Like Hannah, he became suddenly ill while at the Waite residence and died, supposedly of heart disease. Clara, however, had no idea what had really killed her father.

Waite thought about the ghastly secret hiding inside the coffin in the baggage car and how, once again, Clara didn't bat an eye when he relayed her father's wish to be cremated. Following the funeral, he planned to take the body to the same Detroit crematory where Hannah's remains were incinerated. He glanced at the claim check. It was his golden ticket.

There had been a few tense moments when he almost gave away the game. The maid, Dora Hillier, saw him dumping something into John Peck's soup. She easily fell for his explanation that he was giving the old man his medicine. He even asked Dora to taste the soup. Dutifully, she sipped the broth and said she didn't notice a difference, unaware of what it contained. Waite smiled at the thought of the ignorant woman testing his arsenic-laced brew.

They had all been so easy to fool. Arthur Warren Waite grinned as he reached out to hold his wife's hand.

* * *

As Arthur and Clara Waite made the train trek west, a young woman rushed to a Western Union telegraph operator in Grand Central Station. She needed to send an urgent note to Percy Peck in Grand Rapids.[15]

She hesitated before approaching the clerk and wondered if she should meddle in the Peck's family business. She had no evidence, just a female's intuition that something foul had occurred in the Waites' Coliseum apartment. First, Hannah Peck died while visiting Arthur and Clara Waite. Nothing too shocking there; she was infirm. Then, just six weeks later, John Peck died, also while visiting the Coliseum. A husband following his longtime mate's footsteps to the grave was also not entirely unexpected.

Yet John Peck had walked into the Waite apartment healthy and fit and, following the onset of a sudden illness, was carried out feet first. Then, like his wife before him, John's body was going to be cremated. The world of high society was a small one, and she knew people who knew the Waite couple and told her about some pretty odd things associated with the death of John Peck. She shook her head; something was rotten in the Coliseum.

The operator, a middle-aged man with round spectacles, handed the young lady a blank form and a pencil. She jotted out a brief message.

> *To Mr. and Mrs. Percy Peck:*
> *Suspicion aroused Demand*
> *Autopsy Do not reveal telegram*

She paused before adding a name. She wanted to use a pseudonym, but what would be an appropriate nom de plume? She needed something cryptic, something with an allusion that Percy Peck might recognize.

The name "Katherine Adams" immediately came to mind. She had a friend by that name who had recently married.[16] And by sheer coincidence, her friend was the namesake of the victim in one of New York City's most infamous poisoning cases. She remembered reading about the case once.

On December 28, 1898, New York City landlady Katherine J. Adams died minutes after sipping from a cyanide-laced headache remedy given to her by one of her lodgers, Harry Cornish, who received it in the mail from Roland Molineux. Authorities believed that Molineux, a chemist, spiked the Bromo-Seltzer to murder his bitter rival, Cornish. Ignorant of his enemy's scheme, Cornish gave the medicine to his landlady when she complained of a migraine headache. A jury found Molineux guilty after a lengthy trial, but following an appeals court reversal and a second trial, he was acquitted.

She inked the name "K. Adams" and "Coloseum NY" on the form.[17]

"K. Adams" hoped Percy Peck would recognize the sinister allusion.

⸺≫•≪⸺

Percy Peck paced back and forth across the front parlor of Joseph Sprattler's undertaking establishment on Fulton Street. He slid his hand into his vest pocket, pulled out his timepiece and flicked open its lid. Dr. Schurtz would arrive any minute now to begin the postmortem.

The "K. Adams" telegram had beat the Wolverine Express to Grand Rapids. His suspicions piqued, Percy decided to take the advice of "K. Adams" and arrange for an autopsy.

Percy smiled as he remembered the blank expression on Arthur's face. When the train carrying John Peck's body arrived at one o'clock in the afternoon, Percy shocked Clara and Arthur by demanding the baggage checks for his father's corpse. Arthur just stared, dumbfounded, at Percy and Joseph Sprattler, a local undertaker. Percy held out his hand, and Arthur stood, motionless, as the smile melted from his face. Clara didn't know what to make of it but tugged on Arthur's sleeve. Reluctantly, Arthur slapped the papers into Percy's palm.

It was vital that Arthur didn't know about the autopsy, so while Clara and Arthur checked into the Pantlind Hotel, Sprattler took Peck's body to his mortuary. Meanwhile, Percy telephoned the family physician, Dr. Perry Schurtz.

Union Depot in Grand Rapids, Michigan, circa 1900–1910. *From the Detroit Publishing Company, Library of Congress.*

After listening to Percy read the telegram, Dr. Schurtz agreed to conduct the postmortem. He felt all along that something sinister had happened to John Peck. When he heard that Peck had become sick while lodging at the Waite apartment, he urged Percy to go to New York, but Percy was delayed in Grand Rapids by business. By the time he purchased a train ticket, it was too late.

An hour after receiving Percy's call, Dr. Schurtz and Dr. E.P. Billings, a trusted friend who would help him with the autopsy, arrived at the funeral home.

Percy stopped pacing and walked to the door when he noticed the two physicians approaching. Sprattler and Billings looked on as Percy Peck handed the "K. Adams" telegram to Dr. Schurtz, who held the paper up to the light and examined it. He knew no one by the name "K. Adams" but suspected that Dr. Jacob Cornell—a lifelong friend of John Peck—might know something about the mysterious message.

Percy spoke in a hushed tone as he described the mysterious illness that had gripped John Peck. Clara told him that Father became very sick after eating a dish of ice cream and, later, deathly ill after quaffing down a mug of eggnog. "Arsenic," Schurtz whispered as he listened to Percy's narrative. Arsenic poisoning, he noted, shared several symptoms with food poisoning: a sudden onset of nausea, vomiting and diarrhea.

Dr. Schurtz reassured Percy that if John Peck had died from heart disease and nephritis as the death certificate indicated, he would find evidence of it during the postmortem. If Peck had died from ingesting arsenic, he would find evidence of that, too, in the stomach and intestines. He would remove the organs and personally take them to Ann Arbor, where Dr. Victor Vaughn, dean of the University of Michigan's medical school, would conduct an examination and confirm the presence of a heavy metal poison.

———※◦※———

Dr. Schurtz assumed a stoic façade for Percy, but in the back room of the funeral parlor, he felt a tinge of uneasiness. Although a veteran of numerous surgeries, Dr. Schurtz didn't have much experience with postmortems, and now he would conduct one on a man he had known for over thirty-five years.

He stared into the lifeless face of John Peck as he steadied his nerves. An off-white crust at the edges of Peck's mouth hinted at the agony he had suffered during his final moments. The scene was hard to accept; he knew John Peck as a larger-than-life figure, a man who built an empire from scratch.

A small, one-inch scar on Peck's right arm represented the embalmer's work. The undertaker would have pierced an artery and injected about two quarts of embalming fluid. Then, using a foot-long knife called a trocar, he would have made a second incision that pierced the abdominal cavity, allowing the gas and blood to drain out. Once the cavity was empty, he would have pumped in another two quarts of embalming fluid. This simple procedure provided many a poisoner with a forensic alibi until the states began banning the use of arsenic in embalming fluid.

Schurtz took a deep breath as he pressed the edge of his scalpel under Peck's first rib. He drew the blade downward, exposing the deep, red muscle tissue under the pink skin.

After a few minutes, Dr. Schurtz had managed to remove the heart. A close examination revealed no evidence of lesions. As he suspected, the cause of death on John Peck's death certificate was wrong; Peck did not die as the result of heart disease. He handed the heart to Dr. Billings, who slid it into one of the jars, and then began to study the kidneys. Like the heart, the kidneys were unmarked by any sign of disease. John Peck evidently didn't die of nephritis, either.

Peck's stomach, Schurtz thought, showed signs of poisoning. It was contracted into the shape of an hourglass and was fiery red in color. He

Dr. Perry Schurtz, photographed in 1916 during the trial of Arthur Warren Waite. *From the Bain News Service, Library of Congress.*

gently turned the end of the stomach inside out. The inside surface was mottled with dark purple patches where something had eaten away the mucus membrane. Leaning forward, Dr. Schurtz noticed a fine, white powder at the center of each darkened spot. It looked like poison.

With a few swipes of his scalpel, he removed the stomach and portions of the intestines, which Dr. Billings gently placed in jars for transportation to Dr. Vaughn's laboratory in Ann Arbor.[18]

———◦———

While Schurtz conducted the autopsy, Percy returned to the Peck mansion, where he dined with Arthur and Clara. After dinner, John Peck's body still hadn't been delivered to the house for the at-home funeral. Suspicious, Arthur phoned Sprattler and asked him to come immediately.

In the front parlor, Arthur questioned Sprattler about the funeral arrangements. "I personally want a postmortem," Waite remarked, "but my wife will not stand for it." Sprattler just shook his head and told a white lie. He knew nothing about a postmortem, he said.[19]

———◦———

On his way to the Pantlind a few hours later, Waite stopped by Sprattler's mortuary. He wanted to place a picture of Clara and a small flower in the casket. It was Clara's wish, he explained. Sprattler said that the casket was sealed and would under no circumstances be opened.

Waite suspected what had happened. "What is Percy Peck's idea?" Waite barked at the shocked undertaker. "Neither my wife nor I will permit an autopsy."[20] He stomped off without seeing the body.

From the Pantlind, Arthur called Percy and reminded him of John Peck's deathbed wish for a cremation. Percy explained that he wanted to wait before sending the body to Detroit, so his father's many friends had time to pay their last respects. Besides, he added, "friends and family would think it odd if it were rushed to a crematorium."[21]

Percy kept a close eye on his father's body. He arranged to have it escorted to the family crypt at Oak Hill Cemetery and sealed following Tuesday's funeral. He also arranged for a guard to keep a vigil to make sure no one tried to tamper with or even steal it.[22]

———◦———

That evening, Dr. Schurtz took a night train to Ann Arbor, where he delivered the jars containing John Peck's internal organs to Victor Vaughn at the University of Michigan. He and Dr. Vaughn had known each other since Dr. Schurtz graduated from the University of Michigan in 1876. If anyone knew about the effects of poison on the body, it was Dr. Vaughn.

Vaughn picked up the jar containing John Peck's stomach and eyed it. "There's plenty of arsenic there," he remarked.[23] He would confirm his suspicions with the usual battery of tests and prepare a formal report. If he was right—and he was sure that he was—he would eventually need to present the results to investigators and probably to a jury.

Dr. Vaughn explained that if John Peck's organs contained arsenic, it would most certainly not have come from the embalming. New York State, along with Michigan and most other states, had illegalized the use of arsenic in embalming fluids years earlier. That was not to say, he noted, that some old-timer hadn't used antiquated supplies or ignored the law altogether.

The presence of arsenic in John Peck's brain tissue, however, would prove beyond all doubt that he ingested the poison before he died. Therefore, Dr. Vaughn suggested, a second autopsy would be advisable. With a handshake, Vaughn promised to wire the results of his analysis as soon as they became available.

THE PASTOR-TURNED-PRIVATE-INVESTIGATOR

NEW YORK, NEW YORK
Tuesday, March 14–Friday, March 17, 1916

The at-home funeral took place on Tuesday. Family and friends, many of whom had known John Peck for over thirty years, flooded into the front parlor of the Peck mansion, where the business tycoon lay in a chestnut coffin. Dressed in a suit, he looked as if he were taking a nap after an important board meeting. Neither Clara nor Arthur attended the funeral; Clara's nerves had left her bedridden in their Pantlind suite, and Arthur remained by her side.

Ladies attired in black taffeta dresses dabbed their eyes as Reverend Wishart said a few parting words.

Percy waited until after the funeral service to approach Wishart. He wanted to tell him about the postmortem and the mysterious telegram. As attendees shuffled past the coffin to say their farewells, Percy Peck caught the reverend's attention and motioned toward his father's study—a cue Wishart immediately recognized to mean a behind-closed-doors meeting.

As soon as Wishart entered the room, Percy slipped the "K. Adams" telegram into his hand. Wishart studied the scrap of paper as he listened to Percy explain that, according to Dr. Schurtz, the coloring of his father's stomach indicated the presence of arsenic. Wishart didn't recognize the name "K. Adams," either, but whoever this man was, he apparently knew something about John Peck's suspicious death. Wishart vowed to find out as much as he could.

The reverend was not one to let a wrong go uncorrected.

Longtime shepherd of the Fountain Street Baptist Church flock, Wishart began his career behind the pulpit in Trenton, New Jersey. Energetic and opinionated, Wishart purchased a local newspaper, the *Trenton Daily Times*, which he used as a platform to comment on public affairs. The preacher later moved to Grand Rapids, where he continued his personal crusades. He made headlines in 1911 when he attempted to intercede during a strike among furniture workers over wages and length of working shifts.

Wishart felt his heart pounding and his temperature rise. He had once read about a famous sleuth—he didn't remember the name now—who said that during murder investigations, he always first looked to the one with the most to gain from the crime. In this case, that would be the handsome groom whose union to Clara Louise Peck essentially united him with the Peck fortune. It was simple; if she inherited, he profited.

Wishart loosened his collar as he stared out the window at the majestic hardwood trees lining the street. He thought about the New York City he once knew and how it had grown as majestic skyscrapers rose from the streets of Manhattan like iron and concrete trees sprouting through the bedrock underlying the metropolis. He had planned to return one day but never imagined it would be to conduct a murder investigation. So be it. If his longtime friend John Edward Peck had fallen victim to foul play, Wishart would do everything he could to identify the culprit and bring him to justice.

The next morning—Wednesday, March 15—Reverend Wishart and Dr. Perry Schurtz traveled to New York, where they hoped to discover the identity of "K. Adams" and interview key characters in the mystery. As soon as they stepped off the train in Grand Central Station on Thursday, they began tracking down anyone who came in contact with John Peck during his stay in New York.

The armchair detectives interviewed both undertakers, Eugene O. Kane and John S. Potter, and both insisted they followed the law and didn't use arsenic in embalming.[24] Potter, a manager at the Plowright Undertaking Establishment, remarked about how quickly Waite wanted the body embalmed and taken to the train station. There was a haste to it that struck him as odd. It was also strange, Potter recalled, when five hours after the embalming, John Peck's body was still limp. Usually, he explained, rigor mortis would have set in by that time unless the presence of some strong chemical had counteracted the undertaker's magic.

Dr. Schurtz asked for a sample of the embalming fluid. He wanted to bring it to Dr. Vaughn for analysis. Potter turned to Kane, who had handled the actual embalming. Kane explained that he used an old family recipe and would prepare a batch for Dr. Schurtz right away.

Next, they spoke with Dr. William Porter and Dr. Albertus A. Moore.

Porter, who attended Columbia with Dr. Jacob Cornell, said he first saw Hannah Peck two days before she died. "She was very ill," Porter recalled, "showing every evidence of Bright's Disease. I treated her accordingly, but she did not respond to the treatment. I cannot imagine how any intimation gained currency that her death occurred from any other cause." Porter did remark, however, that he considered Hannah's death unexpected.

Dr. Albertus A. Moore, who tended to John Peck from March 4 until his death on March 12, likewise stood by his diagnosis. "The death of Mr. Peck, in my opinion, was caused by nephritis and heart disease," Moore snapped, defensively.

If Vaughn were to find arsenic in John Peck's stomach, Moore said, it did not come from his medicine bag. "During that time, I gave him no medicine that contained even the slightest quantity of arsenic."[25] Like Porter, Moore described John Peck's death as unexpected; although Peck suffered from some type of stomach ailment, he didn't believe it would kill him and was shocked when he heard of his patient's death.

From New York, Wishart and Schurtz traveled to Raritan, New Jersey, where they spoke to Dr. Cornell. The elderly physician, who lived in a large manor with his sisters, Phoebe Swinton and Anna Hardwicke, greeted the two Grand Rapids investigators in the front parlor.

Wishart handed the "K. Adams" telegram to Dr. Cornell, who eyed it suspiciously.

"You and I are both old friends of John Peck," Wishart said, "and I married Clara Peck to Dr. Waite. Tell me, as man to man, did you or did you not send that telegram of warning to Percy Peck?"

Dr. Cornell shook his head. He didn't write the telegram, but he did have his suspicions. His nephew, Arthur Swinton, told him about a curious incident when he bumped into Waite at the Plaza Hotel restaurant. Waite was with an attractive young woman and became flustered when he noticed Swinton enter the room. He told Swinton that he had just performed an important surgery, and this woman was his nurse. After the complex operation, Waite explained, they had decided to take a break for lunch.

Cornell described a visit he made to John Peck on the evening of March 11. Peck appeared "clear eyed," although he complained of a stomachache. Waite had gone to a nearby pharmacy to pick up a prescription for a sedative Dr. Moore had scribed.

When Waite returned, Cornell noticed something peculiar. "Dr. Waite gave Mr. Peck some medicine and soon after, I heard my old friend groan." The next day, he received a call from Clara informing him that Peck had died. "I was shocked because I had satisfied myself that Mr. Peck was gaining in health."

The next day, when he came to pay his respects, he had received an icy reception from Dr. Waite. Cornell found Waite's demeanor so bizarre that he remarked about it to his niece Elizabeth Hardwicke.

Dr. Cornell shrugged. It was probably nothing. An old man's suspicions didn't add up to evidence of wrongdoing.

He then chastised the clergyman. "You know, it is a terrible thing, an awful responsibility for any man to assume—to accuse another human being of murder. Doctor, I want to tell you that no man should ever make such an accusation until he is sure beyond a doubt."[26]

On the afternoon of Thursday, March 16, the surviving members of the Peck family met to hear the reading of John Peck's will.

Percy Peck browsed through a stack of the week's newspapers as he waited for Clara and Arthur to arrive. He nodded as he read the Monday, March 13 headline of the *Grand Rapids Herald*: "JOHN E. PECK, DRUGGIST AND FINANCIER, DIES; PIONEER BUSINESS MAN'S END COMES IN NEW YORK CITY; CONTRACTED COLD ON THE JOURNEY TO THE EAST."[27] No one, not even snoopy news reporters, knew about the autopsy or the covert investigation underway in New York.

He folded the paper and placed it on his lap as Arthur and Clara walked into the front parlor of the Peck manor. Percy couldn't believe his sister's bedraggled appearance. Percy and Ella exchanged a quick glance.

Clara struggled with her emotions during the reading. Several times, she buried her face in her hands. Each time, Arthur wrapped his arms around her shoulders, holding her tight. As he predicted, the Peck fortune passed into equal shares—each worth about half a million dollars—to Clara and Percy Peck. It was the payday Arthur had anticipated. Now, he just had to ensure his complete control over his wife's half.

After the reading, Arthur approached his brother-in-law.

"Percy, we have had a lot of trouble of late. The deaths of your father and mother have been just as big a blow to me as they have been to you, and they have been even a bigger blow to Clara. I hate to think of such things, but I am afraid Clara has not long to live. You know her nervous temperament, and her physical condition, and I am afraid of the future."

Arthur also expressed his concerns about Aunt Catherine, who lived in New York City and had come to know her niece's husband quite well in the past few months. "She is getting along in years and might die anytime. It is terrible that death should stare the Peck family in the face the way it has. It seems so queer. Ever since my marriage to Clara it has been death after death. Where will it strike next?"[28]

Percy tried to keep his emotions in check, but Waite's remark hinted at the imminent danger Clara faced. If Waite was making a play for the Peck fortune, Clara would be his next logical victim.

Arthur hinted that Percy could also be a victim of this strange curse hanging over the Peck family when he chatted with Ella. "You know," Arthur remarked, "I am afraid this is telling on Percy. I have been watching him the last few days, and I can see certain symptoms in him that were so evident in his father's last sickness. I don't want to scare you, but I don't believe he will live six months."

From the Peck estate, Arthur escorted Clara back to the Pantlind. As they walked arm in arm to their suite, Arthur expressed his fears about the deaths occurring around them.

"My dear," he said, "let us talk about our private affairs." His voice was gentle and reassuring. "I am going to take good care of you, but we should try to provide for one another. I think it would be a good thing if I made my will leaving all I have to you and if you would make your will similarly providing for me. Suppose you do it now."[29]

Reluctantly, Clara agreed. She sat down at the writing desk, jotted out a last will and testament on hotel stationery and handed it to Arthur.

Arthur frowned as he read Clara's bequest of almost $40,000 to various charities. He suggested she reduce her charity to half this amount, crumpled up the piece of paper and handed her a fresh sheet.

Obediently, Clara redrafted her will as Arthur dictated, reducing the bequests to $20,000 and leaving the rest to him. She then folded the will and tucked it into an envelope addressed to Waite's lawyer, Archibald Morrison, in New York.

Arthur then suggested they should leave for New York on the next day's train. It would do Clara good to leave Grand Rapids, he said, where memories of happier times lingered around every corner.

Despite Cornell's warning, Wishart believed that Waite had murdered both Pecks, so he turned to the Schindler National Detective Agency for help.[30] On Friday, March 17, he met with super-sleuth Raymond Schindler.

By 1916, Raymond C. Schindler—a protégé of legendary investigator William J. Burns—had acquired a formidable reputation. In 1911, he famously solved the case of a slain child with an ingenious ploy. He staged a murder to occur in front of the prime suspect and fast-talked a newspaper editor into reporting the incident. The suspect, terrified that he would be arrested as an accomplice in the fake murder, blurted out a confession to Schindler's agent.

Schindler listened intently to Wishart's story. He had to hand it to the reverend. He had gone about collecting evidence like a seasoned pro, but unlike Wishart, Schindler wasn't convinced about Waite's guilt. He agreed to join the investigation to find either proof of Waite's scheming or, conversely, proof of his innocence.

Schindler immediately wired Percy Peck, and the two concocted a pretense to keep Clara in Grand Rapids for her own safety. Percy would tell her she needed to remain home to sign some papers before she received her half of the inheritance.

The ruse worked. Arthur didn't want anything to stand between him and Clara's inheritance. So he decided to return to New York by himself. On Friday evening, Clara escorted Arthur to the train station, where he boarded the Wolverine Express.

By Friday evening, Ray Schindler's doubts about Arthur Waite's innocence had begun to evaporate. After discussing the matter with Percy, Schindler spent the rest of Friday afternoon visiting area hospitals in an attempt to find out anything he could. He discovered that Waite was not registered at a single hospital and was not licensed to practice dental surgery in New York. Despite a lack of income, Waite apparently enjoyed a playboy lifestyle. Schindler interviewed dozens of bartenders and maitre d's around Manhattan. Waite was known as a big spender who wined and dined showgirls at nightclubs and restaurants all over the city.

Formidable district attorney Judge Edward Swann, circa 1915. *From the Bain News Service, Library of Congress.*

Schindler became convinced that Waite had murdered both Hannah and John Peck in order to gain control over his wife's inheritance. He phoned Judge Edward Swann, the tenacious district attorney with powerful Tammany Hall connections.

Swann was mildly irritated by the late-night call, but he knew that Ray Schindler would not bother him without good cause. After a few minutes on the telephone, he knew Schindler was on to something.[31]

Swann called a meeting at Wishart's suite at the Manhattan Hotel, where he and his assistant, Francis X. Mancuso, joined Dr. Perry Schurtz, New York medical examiner Dr. Otto Schultze and Raymond Schindler to discuss the case.

When Swann walked into the room, Dr. Schurtz handed him the telegram he had received that afternoon from Dr. Victor Vaughn. It contained one word: "Arsenic."[32]

For the next hour, the men laid out the evidence they had uncovered, but Swann still wasn't entirely convinced. The mass of circumstantial evidence, he admitted, painted an ugly picture of a possible poison plot, but in order to go forward with a case against Waite, he needed something more concrete.

Raymond Schindler knew just where to look.

"SOMEONE IS AFTER ME"

GRAND RAPIDS, MICHIGAN; NEW YORK, NEW YORK

Saturday, March 18–Tuesday, March 21, 1916

With Waite en route to New York, Schindler realized he had a limited window of time. At eight o'clock on Saturday morning, he led a group to the Coliseum, where he cajoled the superintendent into opening the door of the Waite apartment.[33] Inside, the investigators found some provocative clues.

Dr. Perry Schurtz spotted glass slides labeled "typhoid." Waite had apparently devoted a good deal of time to studying dangerous bacteria, which seemed odd for a man not even licensed to practice medicine.

Dr. Otto Schultze found some interesting circumstantial evidence on the bookcase: the second volume of *Woods Therapeutics and Pharmacology*. Familiar with the work, Schultze plucked the book from the shelf and began thumbing through it.

Three strips of yellowed paper were used to bookmark key sections Waite had apparently studied. Pages 331 and 332 contained detailed information about the effects of arsenic on the human system. Pages 158 and 159 contained a discussion of veratria and hellebore. Pages 662 and 663 contained information about expectorants.

As Dr. Schultze dictated his findings, Schindler operative Andrew Taylor penciled the details into a notebook. When he finished, Dr. Schultze slid the book back into its place in the lineup of Waite's medical literature.

Meanwhile, Schindler poked around the bedroom. He stuck his head in the closet where suits, numbering more than one hundred, lined the closet walls. Waite, he mused, was quite the clothes hound.

On the dresser, below a large, oval mirror, he spied photographs of the happy newlyweds. He picked up one of the frames and smiled, wondering if Clara had any idea about the false front her husband maintained.

Feeling something on the back of the frame, he turned it over to discover a small packet of a white, crystallized substance. He dipped his pinkie finger into the powder and tasted it: cocaine. As he eyed the package, he wondered if Waite had fed an overdose to Hannah Peck or if a narcotics habit went along with the high life.

While the others continued to snoop, Schindler installed a bug on the telephone. From this point on, every time Waite picked up the telephone, Schindler's men would be listening.

From the Coliseum, Wishart and Schindler raced to Grand Central Station, arriving just in time to intercept Waite's train, due to arrive at 9:00 a.m. Schindler, who had never seen Waite, wanted the reverend to identify him. Wishart wore a fedora, the brim pulled down over his eyes, so Waite wouldn't spot him.

As soon as the Wolverine Express pulled to a stop in Grand Central Station, Arthur leaped out and raced to a telephone. Schindler kept a few paces behind Waite but didn't take his eyes off his suspect.

When Waite ducked into a phone booth, Schindler went into the adjacent booth and eavesdropped. He heard Waite ask the operator to connect him to the Plaza. A few seconds later, Waite asked for room number 1105. When no one answered, Waite hung up the receiver and wandered around the station. A few minutes later, he returned to the telephone booth and made a second call, but this time Schindler didn't catch the number. He did, however, overhear Waite's end of the conversation.[34]

"Pay the bill, and get out quick," Waite commanded. "I cannot meet you anymore at present because I am being shadowed." He quickly hung up and rushed out of the station with Schindler on his heels.

Schindler and Wishart tailed Waite to the Coliseum in a taxi while Andrew Taylor went to the Plaza to inquire about the guests in room 1105. The clerk handed over the hotel registry and pointed to the name "Dr. and Mrs. A.W. Walters." Taylor showed a photograph of Waite to the clerk, who nodded. "A.W. Walters" was "A.W. Waite."

According to the hotel register, a "Mrs. Walters" had occupied the studio with Waite from February 21 to March 18. The couple registered as "Dr.

The lobby of Grand Central Station, circa 1904. On the morning of March 18, 1916, Reverend Wishart and detective Raymond Schindler began tailing Waite after his arrival in New York. *From the Detroit Publishing Company, Library of Congress.*

New York City's Plaza Hotel. "Dr. and Mrs. A.W. Walters" occupied room 1105 from February 21 until "Mrs. Walters" officially checked out on March 18. *From the Detroit Publishing Company, Library of Congress.*

and Mrs. A.W. Walters," but they used the room only during the daytime, occupying the room for just one night: February 22.[35]

"Mrs. Walters," the clerk noted, had suddenly departed.

Taylor smiled as he connected the dots. This "Mrs. A.W. Walters" was probably the person whom Waite ordered to "get out quick." It was also likely that she was the pretty brunette whom Waite had introduced to Arthur Swinton as his nurse during their chance encounter in the hotel's restaurant. Waite, it appeared, had a second wife.

———

When the elevator opened to the second floor of the Coliseum, Waite found undertaker John Potter waiting for him. After the visit from Wishart and Schurtz, Potter realized that Waite could be in trouble, so he wanted to collect payment for the undertaking work done on John Peck's body.

Waite smiled as Potter asked him for payment, but his smile faded when Potter told him about the investigation taking place. His eyes widened when Potter said that Schurtz had asked for a sample of the embalming fluid.

Waite knew they would find arsenic in John Peck's body. He realized he had one chance to provide a convincing explanation for the presence of the poison. He would bribe the undertaker to say he used arsenic in the embalming fluid. It was a long shot; Waite knew the State of New York had banned its use in embalming years earlier, but if the undertaker agreed to the plan, it just might work.

Waite asked Potter if the embalming fluid contained arsenic. Potter said he didn't know and explained that Eugene Oliver Kane did the actual embalming work. So Waite asked Potter to send Kane to him.

———

On Sunday morning, when he typically would be giving a sermon in Grand Rapids, Reverend Wishart continued to chase down leads in New York. He tried to phone Waite, but he didn't reach him. So he dropped in on Arthur's brother Frank and told a little white lie. Posing as a health officer, he told Frank he needed to speak with Arthur about allegations that Arthur was practicing medicine without a license.

The trick worked. Eventually, Wishart reached Arthur on the phone. He introduced himself as a "Mr. Russell" and told Waite that the health department had received numerous complaints about him practicing without a license.

After a moment of silence, Waite admitted he had never practiced medicine in New York.

"Then you lied to your family and friends?" Wishart asked.

Arthur admitted to lying and went on to explain that when he was supposed to be treating patients, he was, in fact, at the Plaza.

Wishart now realized that Arthur Warren Waite lived a double life. He enjoyed the pleasures of two wives and occupied two residences, but there was one significant similarity: in both lives, he playacted as a practicing physician, when in reality, he didn't even hold a license in the State of New York.

Wishart contemplated Waite's sins as a taxi drove him to the office of the Peck family attorney, Walter Deuel.

Deuel smiled as he watched Wishart enter the room. The reverend wore a fedora and quipped, "The hat is my disguise. I thought I ought to dress for the part."

He briefly described his private investigation in the Big Apple before presenting his written report to Deuel. After he finished reading the report, he felt a deep sense of shame. To expose a liar and a deceiver, he had become one himself. "And may God forgive me for the lies I told and the deceit that I practiced then," he added in a hushed tone.

"You may safely believe He will," Deuel said as he browsed through the handwritten pages of Wishart's investigation notes, the result of what the reverend called "a little detective work."

"I have done more lying since I have been here than in all the rest of my life," Wishart uttered. "I have deceived and I expect I have broken your laws. The Lord forgive me. I did it for what I believe to be the right. I have gone down on my knees and prayed for forgiveness for these sins."[36]

※◦※

On the afternoon of Sunday, March 19, Kane went to see Waite. Nervous and fidgety, Waite asked Kane to detail the chemicals in his embalming fluid. Puzzled, Kane asked Waite why he wanted to know.

"The family is making trouble for me on the other end," Waite said, "and I want to protect myself against them."

Waite listened attentively as Kane rattled off the ingredients of his formula. It did not contain arsenic.

"Could arsenic be put in the embalming fluid?" Waite asked.

Kane nodded. "It could, but I wouldn't do it because it's against the law."[37]

Growing uncomfortable, Kane asked Waite to pay the undertaking bill, but Waite demurred. He said he would send a check later. Kane left the Coliseum empty-handed.

———⟫·◦·⟪———

The next morning—Monday, March 20—Kane phoned Waite to hound him for payment of the undertaker's bill, but aware of the eyes constantly watching him, Waite didn't want to speak on the phone. He ripped off a brief note and sent it to Potter. "Don't telephone me, and don't let Kane telephone me, for the wires are tapped. Don't worry about the check."

Waite slipped out of the Coliseum and phoned Kane from a nearby store. Since his apartment was being watched, he asked Kane to meet him at Cimiotti's Garage on Broadway, where Gustave Cimiotti was fixing his automobile.

A few minutes later, the two men met in a shadowy corner of the garage. Waite handed a check for $9,400 to Kane, who handed it right back.

The tapping of footsteps caused Waite to flinch. He told Kane to pocket the check. "Where can I meet you in an hour and a half?" he asked.

Kane suggested a cigar store at the corner of Ninth Avenue and Fifty-Fourth Street. Waite flashed his million-dollar grin. "I can put you on easy street for life if you do as I tell you." Kane, curious but unsure of what to expect, agreed to the rendezvous and shuffled out of the garage.

When Kane had gone, Waite scribbled out another check for $9,300, but since cashing such a large check would raise eyebrows, he asked Cimiotti to go to the Corn Exchange Bank for him.

Puzzled at the request, Cimiotti told Waite that he wouldn't feel comfortable handling such a large amount.

"That's all right," Waite reassured him, "I just want you to act as my agent and take it around the corner to the Corn Exchange Bank. I am having trouble with my family and am being watched."

Assured that he was doing nothing illegal, Cimiotti agreed. A few minutes later, he returned to the garage with William Lickley, a bank manager, who had come along to make sure the transaction was sanctioned. Satisfied that Waite wrote the check, Lickley led Cimiotti back to the bank to cash the check. Cimiotti then returned to the garage and handed Waite a stack of banknotes.[38]

With a pocket full of cash, Waite headed to the cigar shop to meet Kane.

He slipped into a telephone booth and waited. Kane arrived a few minutes later and entered the booth.

The district attorney, Waite explained, would request a sample of Kane's embalming fluid. He needed it to contain arsenic. If there was a subsequent trial, Waite also needed Kane to testify that there was arsenic in the chemicals he had used to embalm John Peck's body.

Waite shoved a roll of banknotes in Kane's pocket and darted out of the booth.

———<>———

By Monday afternoon, March 20, Waite had become desperate. He knew he was being tailed. Schindler wanted it this way. If Waite knew he was under surveillance, perhaps he would become nervous and slip up, exposing himself.

Waite went to visit Aunt Catherine at the Park Avenue Hotel. For the past six months, Waite had called on John Peck's sister every day. The lonely, seventy-year-old widow, who sat atop a considerable nest egg of her own, craved the attention and was even easier to win over than her sister-in-law, Hannah. Before long, Waite had the elderly woman eating out of his hand. She had even entrusted him with some of her assets, which she asked him to invest on her behalf.

Catherine, aware of the suspicions swirling around her favorite niece's husband, demanded answers. Waite assured her that it was all much ado about nothing.

Aunt Catherine suggested that maybe her brother, in the throes of depression following Hannah's death, took his own life.[39] Waite assured her he would sift this thing to the bottom and kissed her on the cheek. He would call her later, he promised.

Waite had no idea that history was about to repeat itself. Like "K. Adams" before him, he headed straight for the nearest Western Union office to send an urgent telegram to Percy Peck in Grand Rapids. He demanded an autopsy of Father's remains to prove his innocence of any wrongdoing. But unlike "K. Adams," Waite's motive was self-preservation.

———<>———

On Tuesday morning, March 21, Catherine Peck answered a summons to appear in Edward Swann's office. She took a seat in front of Swann's desk and proceeded to detail her relationship with Arthur Warren Waite. Her favorite niece's husband had, in the past year, become like a surrogate son to her. He lunched with her every day, humored her by listening to an old woman's ramblings, entertained her with stories of his adventures and even provided valuable business advice. Swann slowly nodded and whistled when she told him about the $40,000 fortune that she had entrusted to Arthur to invest for her.

Arthur was a good boy, she insisted. She couldn't believe he would have any hand in such sordid business as murder. If it *was* murder—her brother and sister-in-law, she said, were "out of health for some years." She described Hannah Peck as "a great sufferer all of her life." And the previous winter, John had become ill when the family vacationed in Florida—a malady serious enough to land him in New York's Astor Sanatorium.

Still, there were some things about John's death that didn't make sense to Catherine Peck. She described the last time she saw her brother alive: he was wracked by horrific stomach spasms that caused him to wretch and vomit. She recalled that, at the time, the persistent heaving and vomiting puzzled Dr. Moore.[40] There was something else that struck her as a bit odd. "Myself I never heard Brother John express any wish to have his body cremated."

Her eyebrows arched slightly when Swann mentioned arsenic and Dr. Vaughn's findings.

Catherine didn't know how to explain the arsenic found in her brother's remains. She thought it might have been the result of embalming. She said that she believed John Peck regularly took arsenic and could have even been addicted to it, but given John's background as a pharmacist, she couldn't believe it was an accidental overdose.[41]

The discussion with Swann left Catherine Peck conflicted. The DA had raised doubts that began to gnaw away at her confidence in Arthur. She knew of one way Arthur could establish his innocence.

After she left Swann's office, she called Arthur and suggested he also talk with Swann.

———⟫•◦•⟪———

Just after noon on Tuesday, Waite stopped by Swann's office for a brief chat. Swann immediately recognized Waite's ulterior motive: a voluntary appearance in the DA's office, when most criminals would run for the hills, might lend some credibility to his innocence.

Swann got right to the point: doctors had found arsenic in John Peck's body. Waite shifted his weight in the chair and briefly glanced at his shoes. Then he smiled as he thought about the cash he had shoved into Eugene Kane's pocket. Money had a funny way of making people do things.

Swann recognized a hint of confidence in Waite's grin, but it was based on a false hope; the arsenic, he explained, would not have come from embalming. Besides, he noted, his team was headed to Grand Rapids as they spoke and would examine John Peck's brain. If they found arsenic there, murder would be the only logical conclusion.

Waite squinted in his best attempt to appear puzzled.

Swann decided to play along. Who, he asked, might have motive to murder Peck? Did the Peck family have enemies? It was a barbed question that Swann hoped would cut Waite's confidence. After all, Waite had a more powerful motive than anyone else; Swann knew it, and so did Waite.

Waite scratched his head, apparently hard at thought. Swann did his best to keep a straight face. Waite was a good actor, but not that good.

"Percy Peck," Waite said after a few seconds.[42] Waite apparently didn't know or realize the role Percy Peck had played in the investigation. Swann promised to look into it.

With a smile and shrug, Arthur Warren Waite waltzed out of Swann's office like a man without a worry in the world.

It was just an act.

⟶•◦•⟵

From Swann's office, Waite visited the Berlitz School, where he knew he would find "Mrs. Walters."

His appearance shocked her. Arthur didn't look like his usual, happy-go-lucky self. Dark circles around his eyes suggested he hadn't had a good night's sleep in days. And he was nervous. Every few seconds, he looked over his shoulder as if he expected someone to slap a pair of handcuffs on him at any minute.

Like Catherine Peck, she had read the headlines about the mysterious deaths of John and Hannah Peck in the Coliseum. "You didn't do that, did you?" she asked.

"You know I didn't," Waite replied.[43] He explained that detectives were following his every move, but he was certain he had lost them before he went to the Berlitz School.

"Mrs. Walters's" eyes widened when Waite asked her to purchase a large quantity of soporific drugs, but without question, she agreed to follow the doctor's orders. Waite scribbled out a note and handed it to her. She plucked the note from his hand and disappeared around the corner.

A few minutes later, she returned with packages of trional and sulphonal—the powerful sedatives Waite had requested.

Waite cupped her cheeks with his hands and leaned in to kiss her, but she pulled away.

He opened her palm with his left hand while he fished for something in his pocket. Tears formed in the corners of her eyes when he pressed a diamond ring into her palm. The ring was a goodbye gift—a token of Waite's appreciation for the many afternoons they had spent together. Waite managed a smile and left "Mrs. Walters" standing at the curb with her mouth wide open and her face streaked with mascara.

As she watched Waite climb into a taxi, "Mrs. A.W. Walters" slid the ring onto her right ring finger and gently rocked her hand. The diamond glittered.

<hr>

After Arthur left, "Mrs. Walters" sent a delivery boy to the Plaza to fetch some things—personal items she did not want detectives to find.

Ray Schindler was standing in the Plaza lobby when the delivery boy arrived. The boy handed the hotel clerk a note, which authorized the hotel to release "Mrs. Walters's" property to be delivered to the apartment of Dorothy Von Palmenberg. The note was signed "Mrs. A.W. Walters."[44]

The messenger went up to room 1105 to pack up "Mrs. Walters's" things. Thirty minutes later, he left carrying a large suitcase.

Ray Schindler shadowed the messenger to 105 West Seventy-Second Street. When the boy emerged from the building a few minutes later, Schindler approached him. Terrified, he squealed out the details of his errand. Mrs. Margaret Horton, who was a guest of Mrs. Von Palmenberg's, had asked him to pick up some of her things at the Plaza Hotel.

"Mrs. A.W. Walters" had been made.

<hr>

Waite became frantic when he saw the headline "INQUIRY INTO DEATH OF MILLIONAIRE AND HIS WIFE IS BEGUN" in the Tuesday, March 21 edition of the *Evening World*. The article described the official investigation underway. Desperate, he called upon Dr. Albertus A. Moore.

Waite asked Moore if he had kept up on the news about the Peck case. Moore said the entire city was reading about it.

"Do you think they could hold me without an autopsy?" Waite asked.

Moore suggested that an autopsy would remove all doubts, which made Waite even more nervous.

"Do you see that I am suspected?"

Moore, sensing a panic in Waite's voice, suggested that the one way to clear his name would be to demand an autopsy.

"That has already been held," Waite squealed, "and they found enough arsenic in the body to kill two men." He thought for a moment. "Would an autopsy show whether the arsenic was administered before or after death?"

Moore nodded slowly.

"Would it show in the brain? They are going to examine the brain tomorrow."[45]

Once again, Moore nodded and watched, puzzled, as Waite rushed out of the building.

DUALITY

NEW YORK, NEW YORK; GRAND RAPIDS, MICHIGAN

Wednesday, March 22–Thursday, March 23, 1916

Swann's team of New York investigators arrived in Grand Rapids late Tuesday night and checked into two rooms at the Pantlind Hotel.[46]

The man Swann tapped to lead the Grand Rapids end of the investigation, Francis X. Mancuso, headed the homicide department of the New York City prosecutor's office. A large man with broad shoulders, Mancuso was an imposing figure, a trait that served him well in interrogations.

Monroe Street in Grand Rapids Michigan, circa 1910–1915. The Pantlind, where four New York investigators stayed under pseudonyms, is in the background. *From the Detroit Publishing Company, Library of Congress.*

By early 1916, Mancuso had helped bring some notorious characters to justice. He played a critical role in exposing Charles Becker, a crooked cop convicted of murder, and Priest Hans Schmidt, a Catholic priest who cut the throat of his lover, Anna Aumüller. Both Becker and Schmidt took the long walk to Sing Sing's electric chair.

The group met behind the closed doors of room 431 and drafted a plan of action. Dr. Otto Schultze—an expert pathologist—would conduct a second autopsy on John Peck's remains and remove portions of the brain, which he and Dr. Schurtz would then take that afternoon to Dr. Vaughn in Ann Arbor. Any trace of arsenic in the brain would eliminate the possibility that it was the result of the embalming process.

Meanwhile, Mancuso's men would attempt to unearth the real Arthur Warren Waite.

⸺⬧⬧⬦⬦⸺

The grass of Oak Hill Cemetery was covered with silvery dew as assistant superintendent Thomas Sowerby led a crew to the receiving vault at the crack of dawn on Wednesday, March 22.

Sowerby stood a few steps away and watched as four men emerged from the crypt carrying John Peck's chestnut coffin. The silver handles and name plate glittered as the men made their way toward a waiting hearse. As he followed them, Sowerby wondered what secrets the coffin contained. It wasn't every day that a body was removed from Oak Hill, but it appeared that the death of John Peck wasn't an open and shut case after all.

Rumors were circulating, but the investigators from New York—there were four of them—were playing their cards close to their chests. Their trip to Grand Rapids and the disinterment could only mean one thing: they suspected that John Peck died from something other than natural causes.

Sowerby made sure to keep a safe distance as the four men hobbled past him. He was glad they would take the coffin back to Sprattler's mortuary before opening it. After a week, the corpse would be a ghastly sight. The skin would have begun to take on a greenish hue, expanding gases would have caused the torso to bloat and the stench would test the stomachs of even the most stoic.

Medical examiner Dr. Otto Schultze, a slight man with a walrus mustache, turned and followed the casket-bearers to the hearse. Schultze, the big city pathologist who played a key role in exposing some of New York's most insidious poisoners, would go to work in the back room of the Grand Rapids funeral parlor.

As stenographer Nathan Birchall finished typing the investigation report, Francis Mancuso stared out the window of his Pantlind suite and watched as strings of light rain pelted the red brick street below. He thought about the Waite case and the revelations they had uncovered in Grand Rapids. While Dr. Otto Schultze conducted the second postmortem and traveled to Ann Arbor to consult with Dr. Vaughn, Mancuso's men interviewed anyone who knew Waite. In two automobiles Mancuso rented, the New York detectives traveled all over Grand Rapids tracking down leads. Mancuso, who directed the investigation from the Pantlind, also sent cables to Ann Arbor and South Africa. All afternoon, responses flooded into the investigators' suite.

Mancuso spotted a few pedestrians and watched them scurrying under one of the awnings across the street as he pondered Waite's scheme. When it went public, it would become one of the most sensational criminal cases in New York history. Waite's dastardly plot was more spectacular than the sordid crimes committed by Charles Becker, Father Hans Schmidt and Harry Thaw. It certainly would be one of the most shocking cases in the history of this mid-sized midwestern city. Waite, it appeared, had planned to murder at least five Pecks—Hannah, John, Percy, Clara and Aunt Catherine—in a deviously brilliant, get-rich-quick scheme.

Mancuso became so lost in his thoughts that he didn't notice when the pecking of Birchall's typewriter stopped. Birchall tapped Mancuso on the shoulder and handed him a sheaf of papers. It contained the statements of over three dozen witnesses that together unveiled the shocking true biography of Arthur Warren Waite.

Mancuso shook his head as he flipped through the various statements.

Waite, it appeared, had lied, cheated and stolen along the path to life as a bon vivant. Classmates at the University of Michigan related several anecdotes of Waite's petit theft. He swiped money from fraternity brothers, stole dental gold from the university and pilfered money from a summer job on Mackinac Island. He even ripped off the work of fellow dental students and submitted it as his own. In every instance, Waite charmed his way out of any serious consequences.

Somehow, Waite managed to graduate and took a job with Wellman & Bridgeman, a South African firm that recruited Michigan graduates. But the firm required its employees to pass a postgraduate course at the University of Glasgow. The course typically took two years, but to sidestep the requirement, Waite engineered his biggest scam to date. He doctored his paperwork to indicate he had already done a year of graduate work and ended up completing the course in just two months.

Mancuso received a cable from representatives of Wellman & Bridgeman that indicated Waite's sticky fingers continued in Cape Town. He stole dental gold from the company and even opened mail that didn't belong to him. Wellman & Bridgeman would have fired him, but his five-year contract had expired and the war had begun, so Waite left Africa before they had the chance.

Dr. Benjamin Masselink, a doctor from Grand Rapids, worked with Waite in Durban, South Africa. "I knew Dr. Waite was engaged to a girl while in Cape Town, but I could not say whether or not they were married. I know he got into trouble two or three times, and then came back to the United States and entered into practice in New York. Since then I know little of him."[47]

Despite all of this, Masselink said, "I considered Waite a fine man."[48]

Even though his salary over five years never exceeded $15,000, when Waite returned to Grand Rapids in December 1914, he had $20,000 in his pocket and, as Mancuso put it, went "heiress hunting."[49] It didn't take long for him to set his sights on Clara Peck. Once she agreed to marry him, Waite hatched a grandiose scheme to acquire the Peck family fortune.

From her bedside, Clara told Mancuso's men a few anecdotes with sinister implications. Just days before John Peck died, when Waite noticed Clara preparing eggnog, he offered to make it instead. John Peck downed part of the concoction and then began to violently heave. Afterward, Clara spotted flecks of some unknown substance, like partially dissolved tablets, floating in the drink.

It wasn't the first time Clara had noticed something peculiar in a drink that Waite served John Peck. "I saw Dr. Waite put something like them in Father's tea," Clara recalled. "They were about as large as a penny. I don't know what color they were. I saw one dissolving in the bottom of a cup. It changed the color of the tea."[50]

Percy Peck told Mancuso about ominous predictions Waite had made. Following the wedding, he said John and Hannah Peck looked peaked and wondered if they had much time left. Both were in good health, so Percy didn't take Waite seriously at the time, but in retrospect, Waite had briefly showed his hand.

There was something else that bothered Percy: Clara told him that just before Hannah died, her pupils were dilated. This, Percy learned from a doctor friend, was typical of someone who took cocaine, which led him to suspect that Waite had overdosed his mother with narcotics.[51] Waite had ready access to the drug; Schindler had discovered cocaine attached to a picture frame in the Waite apartment.

Mancuso interviewed a friend of the Peck family who asserted that when Arthur spent time with Aunt Catherine, he used whatever pretext he could to besmirch Percy. He apparently had an ulterior motive: he wanted to turn Aunt Catherine against Percy in the hope that she would disinherit him and leave her fortune to Clara instead. Aunt Catherine would then become expendable.[52]

It all added up to one logical conclusion: Waite planned to murder the entire Peck family.

The sun had just begun to drop below the horizon when Mancuso received a telegram from Dr. Otto Schultze in Ann Arbor. Professor Vaughn had finished his examination of the brain tissue taken during the second autopsy on John Peck's remains. He and Dr. Schultze concurred: John Peck had died as a result of arsenic poisoning.

Mancuso rushed to the nearest Western Union office and quickly jotted a message to Swann.

> *Perfect case on present matter.*
> *Prof. Vaughn reports plenty of arsenic*

⇒»·0·«⇐

At about the same time Mancuso wired Swann, Detective John Cunniff sat with the Waites' maid, Dora Hillier, in Swann's Manhattan office. Swann realized that he needed three links in a chain of evidence proving Waite murdered his father-in-law. Dr. Otto Schultze had provided the first link when he concluded that John Peck died of arsenic poisoning. Now, he needed to prove that Waite acquired arsenic and gave it to Peck with malice aforethought. He hoped Dora Hillier would make that connection.

The pretty, young domestic nervously shifted her weight in the chair as Cunniff pulled a notebook and pen from his vest pocket. He nodded, and Hillier began her narrative. Cunniff furiously scribbled notes as the maid described some incriminating things she had witnessed in the days leading up to John Peck's death. Cunniff relayed his conversation to Swann, who requested that Hillier meet him in his office first thing the next morning, where a stenographer could record her story verbatim.

Back in Michigan, at about 5:00 p.m., the Wednesday, March 22 edition of the *Grand Rapids Press* appeared on newsstands. Newsboys across the city yelled out the headline: "POISON IN JOHN E. PECK'S BODY; WAS DRUGGIST MURDERED?"

<hr>

On the morning of March 23, the *Grand Rapids Herald* hit the streets with a headline running from margin to margin: "ARREST IN PECK POISON PLOT MYSTERY IS EXPECTED WITHIN NEXT 48 HOURS; SUSPECT IS UNDER CONSTANT WATCH; CANNOT ESCAPE."

The *Herald* reporter described the crime as "one of the subtlest, and at the same time, most daring poison plots that the criminal history of the country has known."[53]

The headline story included a description of the second autopsy by eyewitness Dr. Perry Schurtz.

"Not only was arsenic found in his stomach (where, it might be argued, it found its way by being a component part of embalming fluid)," Dr. Schurtz said, "but it was found to have affected his brain tissues. That is a certain indication, according to medical men, that the poison was administered before death."[54]

Dr. Schurtz addressed the presence of arsenic in John Peck's remains and explained that New York law forbade embalmers from using it. "Of course, that may or may not mean anything. Laws are violated every day. Arsenic may have been put in the embalming fluid in order to preserve the body. Years ago this poison was extensively used by embalmers, but it is now almost universally prohibited by law."[55]

The news coverage detailed Swann's suspicions that the likely culprit murdered both Pecks and planned a third murder, which would leave him in control of half the Peck fortune. After describing Swann's suspicions, the writer noted that the deaths occurred in the apartment of Mr. and Mrs. Arthur Warren Waite in New York City and that Clara's portion of the fortune was to be held in trust until she turned forty.

The article didn't name Swann's chief suspect, but the implications were clear enough: Arthur Warren Waite poisoned Hannah and John Peck so he wouldn't need to wait thirteen years to come into Clara's half of her father's fortune.[56] Then he planned to do away with her, his third victim.

Most of the Grand Rapids figures in the case avoided the press, but Marie Dille—a *Grand Rapids Herald* reporter—managed an interview with Percy Peck's wife, Ella, who addressed the rumor that Clara made her will at Arthur's request.

This trial sketch by artist J.C. Fireman showing Waite (inset) and Percy Peck's wife, Ella, appeared in the Tuesday, May 23, 1916 edition of the *New York Herald*.

"Mrs. Arthur Warren Waite made her will Thursday evening at the Pantlind Hotel," Ella explained, "just prior to her husband's departure for New York and the beginning of her own illness."

"Do you know in whose favor the will was made?" Dille asked.

"I have not been informed definitely, but I have every reason to believe that it was made in favor of her husband and at his solicitation."

"How did you learn of the will?"

"Clara had told my husband, who informed me Sunday morning, the same day that I am told she was taken ill."

"Have you ever heard Mrs. Waite say that she feared she would die?" Dille asked. "Such a rumor was about town."

Clara's illness had gradually worsened, which some believed was caused by the stress of having lost both her parents. But with Swann's suspicion of a third, unnamed victim, the rumor mill in Grand Rapids had begun churning. What most people assumed was the physical manifestation of a deep grief now took on a new, sinister meaning.

"Yes, yes," Ella said. "A dozen times within the last few weeks I have heard her say she felt that she would be dead inside of a year. She was almost morbid on the subject."[57]

———————————

Dora Hillier arrived at the Coliseum around eight o'clock on the morning of Thursday, March 23, to do her chores. When Cunniff found her, she was standing by the door. She had rung the doorbell of the Waite apartment, but no one answered. She rapped on the door, but still, no one answered.

After assuring Hillier that she wasn't in any sort of trouble, Cunniff escorted her to Swann's office, where she repeated the story she had told the detective Wednesday night. The district attorney listened without interrupting.

"I had been cooking dinner. I had just poured out the soup when Dr. Waite came into the kitchen. He had something in his hand—it was a vial. I had poured out three plates: one for Mrs. Waite, another for her husband and the third for Mrs. Waite's father, Mr. Peck. While I was putting two plates on the tray, Dr. Waite got near the table where the tray was and holding the vial in his hand, poured something from it in the third plate of soup. I did not know what to make of it and I said nothing. With that he—I mean Dr. Waite—said to me: 'This is some medicine for Father.' Then he waited a second or so and said to me: 'Dora, you taste that soup and see whether it is too hot or not. We can't give it to him too hot because his mouth is sore.' I tasted the soup. No, I didn't taste anything funny at all. No, I didn't get sick either. There was nothing peculiar, to my mind.

"After that, I took the tray with the two plates of soup in the dining room and put one plate in front of where Mrs. Waite was seated and the other in front of her husband's place. Then I got the other plate, in which Dr. Waite had poured what I call the prescription from the little bottle I had never seen before, and I put that plate in front of old Mr. Peck. I can't tell whether he tasted the soup or not. He didn't while I was in the dining room.

"About twenty minutes later, Dr. Waite came to the kitchen the second time during the dinner. Shortly before this, I had heard Mr. Peck say in the dining room that he wanted a cup of tea. I was pouring out the tea for the old gentleman already to take into the dining room, when I saw Dr. Waite take the same bottle, or vial, with the stuff in it from somewhere, and he poured some of it into the tea I had just poured out for Mr. Peck.

"'Dora,' said Dr. Waite, 'Father did not like this soup so I will have to put some more medicine in his tea.' And he did so. After Dr. Waite had finished his pouring I put some cream into the tea for Mr. Peck and placed the cup in front of Mr. Peck in the dining room. I don't know whether he took any of the tea or not. I was pouring a second cup of tea for Dr. Waite. His wife did not care for any that evening. That is all I know about that."

Hillier, though, had never seen Waite spike Hannah Peck's food. "Mrs. Peck had a nurse," Hillier explained, "and Mrs. Waite was with her mother all the time and looked after her herself. I guess that is why I didn't see anything."[58]

Dora Hillier couldn't help Swann make a case for Hannah Peck's murder, but she had provided an important link in a chain of evidence connecting Waite to John Peck's murder. Peck died from arsenic poisoning, and Hillier saw Waite spiking John Peck's food with some unknown substance. Although Hillier hadn't identified the substance as arsenic, Swann was sure he could convince a jury *if* he could find evidence that Waite had purchased the poison. That left just one missing link: Swann needed to prove Arthur had purchased arsenic. He had to find the pharmacy.

——→◦←——

Mancuso unfurled the December 11, 1914 edition of the *Grand Rapids Press* that one of his investigators had unearthed in the newspaper back files. The paper contained an article detailing the successful dental career of Arthur Warren Waite, published when Waite returned from South Africa. The assistant DA smirked as he read the interview in which Waite gloated about his academic success at Harvard and London Universities before he attended the College of Royal Surgeons in Edinburgh, Scotland, on a scholarship. It was a tissue of lies.

By midmorning on Thursday, March 23, Mancuso had done about all the digging he could in Grand Rapids. He had unmasked Arthur Warren Waite as a charlatan and uncovered evidence of a twisted plot that, if it wasn't for the "K. Adams" telegram, would have certainly spelled doom for Clara and possibly Aunt Catherine and Percy Peck.

Before Mancuso returned to his suite at the Pantlind to face the press, he needed to send one final telegram to Swann. Mancuso penciled in the message and handed it to the Western Union clerk.

The clerk's mouth dropped open as he read the message:

> *Arrest Waite immediately*
> *Evidence of guilt overwhelming*
> *Obtained substantial amounts of money on false pretenses*
> *Check up bank accounts and hold up all deposits*

Swann smiled as he reread the first two lines of Mancuso's telegram.

"Arrest Waite immediately. Evidence of guilt overwhelming."

He ordered Detective Cunniff to find Waite and arrest him for murder. Cunniff made a beeline to the Coliseum.

Frank Waite answered the door. About an hour earlier, he had entered the apartment and found Arthur groggy and fading fast. He had downed a handful of sedatives. Frantic, Frank raced to the phone and called Dr. Moore, who arrived a few minutes later.

Frank described the scene as Cunniff eyed Waite lying motionless on a bed in a backroom of the palatial apartment.

"A stomach pump! A stomach pump!" Arthur had wailed in agony as the sulphonal and trional began to overwhelm his system.

Moore then asked him when he took the drugs.

"At eleven o'clock this morning, I began," Waite managed to squeal in between gasps. "I had to get some sleep."

"How much have you taken?" Moore asked as he fished in his bag for something to counter the overdose.

"Plenty," Waite mumbled as he fell back into a semicomatose state.[59] He had been in that condition for over an hour when John Cunniff came to arrest him.

By Thursday evening, March 23, Catherine Peck found herself in the midst of a media frenzy.

As the story progressed, it became evident that Aunt Catherine had unwittingly financed Dr. Waite's playboy lifestyle. With her money, he funded his affaires de coeur, cavorting with showgirls and cohabitating with "Mrs. Walters."

Reporters also alleged that Aunt Catherine had narrowly missed becoming the first Peck poisoned by Arthur Warren Waite. After transferring her funds into his accounts, it appeared, Waite began to systematically plan for her death. No one would question the sudden illness of an elderly woman, and her demise would serve two purposes: he could use her as an experimental dummy, and he could avoid any possible questions about the purloined $40,000.

Reporters, hoping to interview Waite's benefactress, swarmed the Park Avenue Hotel. One of them finally managed to eke out a statement. Aunt Catherine found the malignant plotter imagined by the press to be so incongruous to the Arthur Warren Waite she knew that it was impossible to believe.

"All I know about our transactions is this: that I gave him the money and securities—I should say that $100,000 was too high perhaps—and asked that he invest them. I considered him perfectly trustworthy and reliable, and when he said he had invested my money I took it for granted that he had. I did not question him or ask him to show proof of his statements. Some of the securities I gave him to find out their value, and not invest."

The reporter listened as Catherine Peck discussed how Arthur had managed to fool the entire Peck family. With the news leaking out of Grand Rapids, Aunt Catherine was embarrassed by how in the dark she was about Waite's duality.

"I always thought Dr. Waite was one of the purest-minded men I ever knew. I never heard one foul or mean word fall from his lips. No one was so astonished when I found that he had been living with a woman at the Plaza. I have also heard that he has been frequently seen with other young women about town. But he kept all this side of his life well hidden from his family. His wife never had the slightest suspicion that he was not faithful to her. Why, she was as happy as the day was long. She was always going around the apartment singing and dancing. She was so sure of his entire love."

Aunt Catherine shook her head. "I can't understand this at all. If Dr. Waite had needed money he could have had it for the asking from his wife's family. We were all very proud of him. We considered him a brilliant man and were proud of his successes."[60]

With reporters camped out in the lobby of the Pantlind, Francis X. Mancuso realized he had to issue some type of statement, so he invited them to his suite on the evening of March 23. Newspaper reporters from both the *Grand Rapids Press* and the *Grand Rapids Herald* joined three correspondents from New York and another three from Chicago who had followed the story to Michigan. By this point, Arthur Warren Waite had become big news.

Mancuso paced the room as he spoke, choosing his words carefully. The reporters jotted down his every word in their notebooks.

"Arthur Warren Waite is guilty of the murder of John E. Peck. We have positive proof against him and in all my experience in criminal matters," Mancuso added, "I have never been more confident of a conviction than in this case." To readers of the mid-sized midwestern metropolis, this was a startling statement coming from the head of New York City's homicide department.

"We have an open and shut case against this man," Mancuso gloated. He explained that the two days his team had spent in Grand Rapids had led to damning evidence against Waite. He added a teaser: "The case so far has been a sensation, but the biggest sensation is yet to come. Before we are through with this case we will have uncovered one of the greatest poison plots in criminal annals."

Mancuso paused as the reporters furiously scribbled notes. "Waite is one of the most desperate of men," he continued. "He would stop at nothing to get his hands on money. He needed it. He was living a life in New York City that cost him $50,000 a year. He did not work."

The reporters stared at Mancuso in disbelief. Waite was a well-known dentist in New York. He even took Clara with him to the various hospitals where he conducted dental surgeries.

Sensing their confusion, Mancuso said, "Where did the money come from? When this question is answered the sensation of an age will be known."

Mancuso then detailed the true biography of Arthur Warren Waite, the biography behind the debonair façade.

Waite, Mancuso said, did work for a dental firm in South Africa and, despite allegations of theft, managed to squirrel away a considerable sum of money. When he returned to the United States, he presented himself as an expert in oral surgery to physicians throughout the Big Apple. "He claimed to have performed some of the most difficult feats known to oral surgery, when in fact he had never performed one.

"This," Mancuso continued, "was the beginning of his dual personality."

Mancuso detailed Waite's double life. Waite didn't perform surgery, didn't tend to patients at hospitals and didn't even maintain an office. Instead, he spent his afternoons at the Plaza Hotel, where, Mancuso said, he had "installed a Mrs. A.W. Walters there as his wife."

The reporters gasped.

When Waite wasn't busy playing with "Mrs. A.W. Walters" at the Plaza, he played tennis. His skill on court led him to a championship at Madison Square Garden and a top twenty ranking for all male tennis players in the country.[61]

Mancuso also commented on Waite's likely choice of attorney. Rumor had it that he would hire John B. Stanchfield, the celebrated defense attorney who had won an acquittal for accused murderer Harry Thaw. Mancuso had squared off against Stanchfield several times in court and knew him as a top-notch criminal attorney.

"Waite's defense will cost him a fortune. Stanchfield is the best criminal lawyer in New York. He never takes a case unless he has a $10,000 retainer, and he would not handle a case like this for less than $50,000."[62]

Mancuso fielded a few questions from the curious reporters.

One reporter asked if Waite was suspected of other New York crimes, such as the mysterious death of a wealthy New York widow.

Irritated, Mancuso refused to answer the question.

Another reporter asked if Waite had committed bigamy. "Do you know whether Dr. Waite has a wife in South Africa?"

"I don't think he has. He was engaged to a girl there, but when her parents learned of his character, the engagement was broken off."

"Has he a wife in New York?"

"Not that I know of, although he was living with this Mrs. Walters as his wife." Mancuso described her as a society woman but didn't elaborate. He said he didn't know her exact whereabouts.

Intrigued by Waite's extramarital affairs, another reporter asked Mancuso about a rumor that had been floating around. "Was Waite engaged to the daughter of a New York millionaire with whom he played tennis in an indoor tournament in Madison Square Garden recently?"

"I can't say that he was engaged to her. His name and hers have been used together, but because of her position in society, I would not feel free to give her name."

"Do you think other members of the Peck family were included in the poison plot?"

"I can't answer that. I will say this, however, that this man would go to any extent to get money."

Celebrated defense attorney John B. Stanchfield, who successfully represented Harry K. Thaw and secured his release from Matteawan. Authorities originally believed that Waite would hire Stanchfield to represent him. *From the Bain News Service, Library of Congress.*

When asked about the important evidence uncovered in Grand Rapids, Mancuso refused to divulge specifics. He didn't want to give away their case. The reporters continued to pelt Mancuso with questions.

"Are there any women involved in this end of the case?"

"Not that I can tell you of."

"Is it a fact that you have had before you a prominent local woman who was very friendly with Waite?"

Mancuso stared at the reporter in silence.[63]

He concluded the interview by praising two gentlemen from Grand Rapids for their tenacity in exposing the plot.

"The entire credit must go to Dr. Wishart and Dr. Schurtz. These two men conducted an investigation for two days in New York, assisted by private detectives, and when they placed the case before us, we were ready to act. When we came here, Dr. Wishart took off the lid—he uncovered one of the most startling crimes I have ever heard of."

Their efforts, Mancuso concluded, "will furnish a story that has not even been rivaled by the fertile imaginations of the most prolific fiction writers."[64]

CONFESSION

NEW YORK, NEW YORK

Friday, March 24, 1916

In Grand Rapids, Arthur Warren Waite had become headline news. The entire front page of the Friday, March 24 edition of the *Herald* was devoted to the Peck case. Under the headline "Coils of Guilt Tighten About Waite," staff writers speculated about Waite's dark motives.

"Grand Rapids society is still trying to catch its breath from the shock it received with the arrest Thursday of Dr. Arthur Warren Waite, and the revelation of his double life and Dr. Jekyll and Mr. Hyde existence," wrote a correspondent for the *Grand Rapids Herald*.[65]

In New York, Edward Swann contemplated the "coils" around Arthur Warren Waite's neck. There was one vital link missing: Swann needed proof that Waite purchased the arsenic he used to poison John E. Peck.

The sun had barely risen on Friday morning, March 24, when Swann sent teams of investigators across Manhattan in search of the missing link.

Waite, Swann reasoned, must have purchased it somewhere near one of his two homes: the Coliseum or the Plaza. He sent teams to both locations with orders to canvass the pharmacies closest to these two spots and work their way outward in radiating spirals.

Swann also sent Assistant District Attorney John T. Dooling to the Fifth Avenue Bank to seize Waite's safety deposit box.

By midmorning, both teams would make major discoveries.

As Swann's investigators turned Manhattan upside down for the pharmacist who sold Waite arsenic, Warren and Sarah Waite boarded a Metropolitan train to New York. They wanted to see their son before it was too late.

While the train began rolling out of Grand Rapids, Warren glanced at his pocket watch: it was 10:30 a.m.

Warren unfolded the note his daughter-in-law had given to him earlier that morning. Too ill to travel, Clara wanted to send a message to Arthur.

Warren's eyes misted as he read the note.

"Father, tell my darling husband that I love him with all my heart. Tell him I want to come to him, to be with him, to cheer him, to comfort him in his great trouble. Tell him I do not believe one word of all that has been said about him. Say to him that no matter what happens, I shall always be his loving wife. Tell him, please, that the happiest moments of my life have been spent with him. I love him, oh, ever so much."

Clara promised she would come to New York as soon as she felt well enough. She also told Arthur not to worry about the reports of his "other woman."

"And please say to him that I have heard what they have said about him and another woman. It makes absolutely no difference to me. And even if it were true about that other woman, tell him that I forgive him, because I realize that the other woman had in her mind to destroy our happiness. She must have been a woman who simply would not give up my Arthur."[66]

Clara ended her request: "Give him my undying, eternal love. Kiss him for me."

Clara didn't deserve all of this, Warren thought as he folded up the note and put it in his jacket pocket. The truth had always been a stranger to his son.

He felt a knot in his stomach. What if everything he read in the papers was true?

⇒►◦◄⇐

As his parents boarded a train in Grand Rapids, Arthur awoke from his thirty-six-hour, drug-induced stupor.

"Who is that man, and what is he doing here?" Waite groaned, pointing at one of the men Swann had sent to look after his number one suspect.

"They're with the district attorney," John Cunniff replied as he knelt down next to Waite's cot.

"Good God, man, I've got to get this thing off my mind! I've got to tell somebody something. I want my wife. Where's Clara?"

Clara, Cunniff reminded Waite, was still in Grand Rapids. He asked if there was anything he could do.

"You can't help me! I'm the worst scoundrel on the face of the earth. The whole world is against me!"

"We've all made mistakes," Cunniff said.

"Yes, but I've been found out."[67]

Realizing that Waite might be ready to talk, Cunniff telephoned Swann, but he was out of the office, so George Brothers raced to the apartment. When he arrived, however, Waite had become tight lipped.

Frustrated, Brothers marched out of the Coliseum.

In the vault of the Fifth Avenue Bank, Dooling fingered through the contents of Waite's safety deposit box.

Skimming through the dozens of documents, Dooling was able to trace what had happened to Catherine Peck's $41,000 in cash and $100,000 in securities.[68]

Waite took most of the cash and the stocks—shares in a petroleum company, the Brooklyn City Railroad, gold and silver mining companies and others—to the brokerage firm of Spaulding, McLellan & Company and opened a portfolio in his name. Waite then used the purloined stocks to begin a run at stock speculation.

Like his tennis game, he liked to play fast and quick with Aunt Catherine's money, buying and then selling in the hope of fast profit. Either he lacked the patience of a long-term investor or he wanted to cash in quickly. Dooling remembered hearing that Waite fantasized about purchasing a castle in Italy. Prince Charming, he mused, probably intended to finance his dream home with money from Aunt Catherine.

One set of documents puzzled Dooling. Just a few days earlier, Waite had sold one hundred shares, raising $9,480, and used the money to open an account with the Corn Exchange. Then, suspiciously, he withdrew it.

The box also contained correspondence with other women, most of them Broadway dancers. Dooling read through a few of the letters, but it felt like eavesdropping, so he put them aside.[69]

Another set of papers piqued Dooling's interest: dated from December 21, 1915, to March 7, 1916, they related to the acquisition of dangerous bacteria. It appeared that Waite, masquerading as a research scientist, purchased germ samples from several area laboratories.

Dooling immediately realized the significance of these documents. In a memo to Swann, he characterized the bacteria as "sufficient to kill many persons and which could be administered in liquids, such as soup, tea, etc." The date sequence indicated that Waite may have acquired deadly agents almost three months before John Peck's murder and had them in hand well before the death of Hannah Peck in January 1916. The last date in the sequence was just days before John Peck's death.[70] The use of disease germs would have made for a perfect murder; an autopsy on a person who died of pneumonia or typhoid would reveal nothing more than a natural cause of death.

Dooling slid the papers into his valise and headed back to the office.

As soon as he arrived, he phoned Walter Drew, Catherine Peck's attorney. If Drew acted quickly and took action to freeze Waite's accounts, he might save his client from financial ruin.

⟶➤◆⟵

For two hours, investigators canvassed pharmacies closest to Waite's apartment and the Plaza Hotel. It was midmorning when Detective Frank Gallagher struck pay dirt on Lexington Avenue.

In a brief conversation with the proprietor, druggist Richard Timmerman, Gallagher learned that Waite had purchased arsenic from his store in early March.[71] Waite, unable to acquire the drug himself, asked for the help of his physician, Dr. Richard Muller. He told Muller that he wanted to get rid of some pesky cats. Dr. Muller in turn contacted Timmerman, who agreed to make the sale.

Timmerman called for his clerk, Richard C. Schmadel, who remembered the incident quite clearly. Timmerman had asked him to weigh out ninety grains and make out a receipt.

Schmadel opened the poison register Timmerman used to record all purchases of dangerous substances and thumbed through the pages until he found the entry for March 9. There it was, he said, in Waite's handwriting. He handed the open book to Gallagher, who read the entry. It contained the date of purchase, the name of the buyer, the amount of poison and the notation "To kill a sick cat."[72]

Gallagher had found Swann's missing link. He raced to the DA's office with the ledger under his arm.

When Gallagher arrived, Swann was poring over a letter he had received from E.H. Williams, a New York tailor John Peck often employed to custom-make his suits. According to Williams, when Peck visited his store on February 23, he complained of stomach cramps after eating pistachio ice cream at his son-in-law's apartment the night before. Peck thought he was suffering from food poisoning. "I advised Mr. Peck to see a physician," Williams said, "but he said he had no great confidence in medicine, that his son-in-law had given him some medicine but no relief from pain had followed."[73]

Swann read the ledger entry and smiled. His detectives had just found Waite's "medicine." He shook Gallagher's hand and reached for the telephone. He needed to speak with John Cunniff.

Detective John Cunniff had just dozed off in a chair when the apartment telephone rang. It had been a long shift. Since he had entered the Waite apartment the day before, he had kept a constant vigil over the suspect.

Swann told Cunniff about Gallagher's discovery and ordered him to confront Waite with this new evidence. "Let Waite know about this," Swann said. "Tell him all we've learned. Let him think it over. I shall be up presently."

Cunniff walked to the back room where Waite lay in bed. He folded his arms across his chest and eyed the suspect. "Well, doctor, they've got some pretty strong stuff on you. The doctor and the druggist through and from whom you got the arsenic have told the district attorney all about it. Now, hadn't you better make a clean breast of the whole business? The judge even has the receipt you signed when you got the arsenic."

"Not true!" Waite howled. "Not true! It's a lie."

"All right. If you don't want to talk to me will you talk to the district attorney?"

Waite nodded. "Yes. I'll see him. He's been very decent to me."[74]

Waite lay in bed with a blue comforter drawn up to his chin and watched as District Attorney Swann, followed by Assistant District Attorney George N. Brothers and a stenographer, walked into the room at about 3:00 p.m. Waite held out his hand, and Swann briefly grasped it as he studied the pathetic figure. Waite's handshake was limp, his hand cold and clammy.

Swann was shocked at Waite's appearance; haggard, pale and with black bags under his eyes, Waite looked like a shadow of the confident, grinning man about town whom he had first met in his office just two days earlier.

That man, who chuckled when the DA told him he was a suspect in a possible murder plot, looked nothing like the pathetic figure lying on the cot in front of him.

New York detectives Bernard Flood and Cunniff, along with Ray Schindler and a nurse, stood by Arthur as Swann began his questioning.

"Doctor," Swann began, "did you buy arsenic in a drugstore in the early part of this month?"

In a weak, trembling voice, Waite answered. "Yes, I did—powdered arsenic in a paper."

"Is this your signature to the receipt for that arsenic?" He held out the receipt so Waite could see it.

"Yes, sir, it is."

"What did you buy it for?"

Waite managed a slight smile. He wondered what Aunt Catherine would say if she knew she had unwittingly supplied him with an alternative explanation for Peck's death when he visited her on Monday.

"I'll tell you, but you won't believe me. My father-in-law was an old man and very despondent since the death of his wife. He told me that with her gone he did not want to live any longer and wanted me to get him some poison that would kill him. I am not sure that he said what kind of poison he wanted, but he must have mentioned arsenic, because I bought arsenic. This was about three days before he died."

Swann nodded in agreement. At least Waite's timeline matched the documents. "Our receipt bears the date of March 9, and it was on March 12 that Mr. Peck died."

Waite continued. "I went to this doctor and told him that I wanted arsenic. I asked him to tell his druggist to give it to me, and he telephoned him. I went around to the druggist, gave him my name and after some little conversation I got the arsenic in powdered form. I brought the arsenic home with me and gave it to Mr. Peck. I didn't ask him if he had, but if you found arsenic in his stomach he must have taken it. I'm sorry I didn't die myself; you've got the law on me, and I expect I'll go to the electric chair because I can't prove what I say. I'm sorry I didn't die when I took that stuff. How much of it did I take?"

"I'm sure I don't know," Swann replied flatly.

"Well, I took a lot."

"How did you give the arsenic to Mr. Peck?"

"It was in powder form, and I gave it to him in the original package the day I bought it."

Waite spoke with very little inflection in his voice and no apparent emotion—a reaction that Swann found extremely odd under the circumstances. Most suspects, in his experience, reacted to such serious accusations with emotions that ranged from indignation to downright panic. Then again, Waite was apparently still dazed from the overdose.[75]

"What did Mr. Peck say when you gave it to him?"

"He merely took it. He never said whether he swallowed any of it, and I never asked him. He wanted me to get it for him, and I did." Waite noticed Swann's expression. Clearly, he hadn't convinced the DA. "Oh, I know you don't believe me."

Swann studied Waite, and the two eyed each other in silence.

"What do you think Mr. Peck was worth?"

"I know—$1 million. He had a great deal of real estate and many securities besides."

"Did your wife, did anybody, know about your buying this poison?"

"No, no, my wife didn't know about it, and I don't want her to know. My great regret is how this will wound her. No, no one knew about this but myself. You won't believe me, I know, and I suppose I'll have to go to the electric chair." Waite paused as looked around the room. He spotted the stenographer who was standing in the corner, furiously scribbling notes on a notepad. "You needn't stand over there," he said to the stenographer, who briefly took his eyes off the notebook and glanced at Waite. "You can come right out here. I know you've got me."

Swann resumed his interrogation: "What about the $40,000 your aunt turned over to you?"

For the first time during the interrogation, Waite showed some anger. "What has that got to do with the subject in hand?" he snapped.

"You carried a speculative account, didn't you?"

"I wouldn't call it that. I bought outright—New York Central, Pennsylvania and stocks like that."

"Did you buy on margin at any time?"

"Yes," Waite said slowly, "I did buy some on margin."

"Did you carry your account to a loss?"

"I don't know yet."

"Did you hesitate when Mr. Peck asked you to buy the poison?"

"No, I didn't. He said he didn't want to live any longer and that he wanted me to get some poison that would kill. So I got it. Oh, I know you won't believe me, and I suppose I'll have to go to the electric chair."

Swann shrugged. He had what he needed for now. Waite had admitted to buying the arsenic. As Swann stood up to leave, Waite said, "I want you to tell me something." Swann stopped and turned toward Waite, who propped himself up on his elbows. "What would you do if you were in my case?"

"I can't conceive myself in your case."

"Oh," Waite said with a tone of resignation, "I was an ass; there's no doubt about that. What are you going to do to me?" Waite asked.

Swann said that he would leave Waite in his apartment until he was strong enough to be moved to Bellevue Hospital. Waite said he didn't want to leave, but Swann glanced at the window next to the bed and realized that Waite could easily jump before Cunniff caught him. He didn't want his suspect to cheat the hangman.[76]

As Swann and Brothers left the room, Frank Waite asked them what Arthur had said. Frank listened, his eyes widening slightly, as Swann recounted the interview.

The district attorney said that Arthur seemed to be under the impression that if he could establish he helped John Peck commit suicide, he would be in the free and clear. But, Swann explained, even if he had, he would still be guilty of first-degree manslaughter and facing a possible twenty-year prison sentence.

When Swann noted that Arthur had said more than once he expected to go to the chair, Frank Waite looked like someone had just socked him in the stomach. Tears began to flow down his cheeks, and he wiped them away with the back of his sleeve in a way that moved the district attorney. It was a pyrrhic victory. Swann knew the tremendous burden such a case places on the loved ones left behind to figure out where it all went wrong.

Back in the small room, while Swann briefed Frank Waite, Arthur made one final attempt to cover his tracks.

He called Schindler to his bedside.

"Do you think they will use against me what I have told them?" Waite asked.

"Well," Schindler replied, "you have several things you'll have to explain. One is that you didn't give your father-in-law the arsenic without his knowledge."

"I handed it to him in the original package."

Schindler immediately recognized an opportunity to trap Waite into making an incriminating move. "Did your wife or your maid see you do it?"

"No, but we could say someone did. Would you do something for me? Would you see Dora Hillier and get her to say she saw me hand the package to the old man, but that she hadn't known I knew she had seen me?"

Schindler decided to bait the hook. "She wouldn't do that."

"She would if she were paid. I'd pay her $1,000."

"Where would I get the $1,000 to give her?"

"I have $15,000 with Spaulding, McLellan & Co., and I'll give you an order for $1,000."

Schindler couldn't believe Waite had taken the bait. He had played it perfectly. He ripped a piece of lined paper from his notebook and handed it to Arthur.

"I can't write," Waite said. "You write it and I'll sign it."

As Waite dictated, Schindler wrote out the order. When he finished, he handed the page to Waite, who scrawled his name at the bottom and handed it back to Schindler. The stunned detective studied it for a few seconds.

Ray Schindler couldn't believe his eyes. In all his years on the job, he had never before seen anything like it—a suspect attempting to use one of the investigators in a scheme to fabricate evidence.

Schindler carried the message to Swann, who smiled when he read Waite's feeble attempt. Waite didn't know that while he lay in a coma, Hillier had testified to the grand jury that she watched Waite dump some unknown substance into John Peck's food just before his death.

⇒·◦·⇐

On Friday night, March 24, the best show in New York City took place behind closed doors where an *Evening World* reporter conducted an interview with the city's newest celebrity. After the reporter had identified "Mrs. A.W. Walters" as Mrs. Margaret Horton, a married singer from Ohio, a new chapter to the already-twisted story began.

"Mrs. A.W. Walters" wanted to clear up allegations floating around about her role in Waite's scheming. Just the day before, an *Evening World* correspondent had reported that Swann suspected her relationship with Waite predated Waite's marriage to Clara and wondered if Waite hadn't planned the murders so he could run away with her. And then there was the fact that she had left the Plaza very quickly after receiving a telephone call from Arthur, suggesting that Arthur, suspiciously, wanted to keep her away from the authorities for some reason.[77]

The *Evening World* reporter stared wide-eyed as the beautiful brunette, her husband in tow, sashayed across the room and sat down in the chair opposite him. She crossed her legs, folded her gloved hands in her lap and pursed her lips in an attempt at a smile. She was nervous. She tilted her head and waited for the first question.

The reporter asked her to describe her background and how she had come to meet Arthur Warren Waite. Margaret cleared her throat and began her narrative.

Juliet to Waite's Romeo: Mrs. Margaret Weaver Horton, who spent time with Waite at the Plaza Hotel under the assumed name of "Mrs. A.W. Walters." A *Sun* staff photographer snapped this photograph of Waite's "studio companion" a few days after her six-hour interrogation with Dooling. *From the* New York World-Telegram *and the* Sun Newspaper *Photograph Collection, Library of Congress.*

She was born Otila Margaret Weaver in Cincinnati, Ohio, in December 1892. The daughter of a traveling salesman, she lost both of her parents at a young age and was living at a boardinghouse when thirty-six-year-old Harry Mack Horton first met her. Just four days later—on Valentine's Day 1914—Horton married the twenty-one-year-old "Tillie" Weaver. They later moved to New York City, where Margaret dreamed of a career on Broadway.

Her relationship with Arthur Warren Waite, she said, began one fateful afternoon when, instead of performing dental surgery, he attended a performance at the Academy of Music, where he spied Mrs. Horton on stage. He became enamored with the stunning contralto, and she admired his passion for the arts. With similar interests in music and drama, they began to study together. Their relationship evolved, eventually leading to a room at the Plaza Hotel, where she spent many afternoons with Waite.

Margaret insisted the relationship was platonic and said she knew nothing about the pseudonym Waite had given her at the hotel. They spent their time together studying, nothing more.

"Dr. Waite rented a studio at the Plaza, where we studied music, singing, and languages in the afternoons. It was just the same as renting a studio in any building along Fifth Avenue. He put in a piano and brought in two bags of books and pictures. Neither of us ever spent the night in the room—in fact, there was no bed in it."[78]

Margaret stood by Waite despite the mounting evidence against him.

"I believe in Dr. Waite absolutely. Even now I cannot believe he is guilty of the crime of which he is accused. It seems utterly unthinkable. He appeared to me so frank, so carefree. There was no concealment about our acquaintance. We went to and from the room in the Plaza as openly as if we had been walking on Fifth Avenue, for there was not a thing to conceal."

Margaret did everything she could to characterize Waite as a brother, not a lover.

"Dr. Waite often spoke to me about his father-in-law and expressed great affection for him. He said Mr. Peck's health had declined since his wife's death and that he seemed to be suffering a good deal. He always spoke of Mrs. Waite with the greatest love and respect, and often expressed the hope that Mr. Horton and I should come to see them."

She paused and took a sip of water before continuing.

"On the other hand, I was just as open and free about Dr. Waite. I told Mr. Horton of our studies together in Dr. Waite's studio, and Mr. Horton offered no objections. Many times I urged Dr. Waite to come down to our apartment, but there was always some engagement to prevent his coming."[79]

Harry Mack Horton backed his wife's story. "I knew of Dr. Waite and that he and Mrs. Horton were studying music and language together. Mrs. Horton told me Dr. Waite had invited her to go to his studio in the Hotel Plaza, and I gave her my full permission to do so."

Horton went on to describe his wife as a simple country woman—naïve and easily controlled by a schemer like Waite. "At an early age," he said, "she lost her father, mother, and brother...In a great many respects, as anyone who knows her will agree, she is about fifteen years old in her knowledge of worldly things."

Horton discussed how he had found out that his wife was playacting with an infamous murder suspect: a newspaper reporter had cornered him with the possibility.

"I know that my wife has been studying with a Dr. Waite or some name like that," Horton told the reporter, "but I don't connect it with this Dr. Waite in the newspapers." Bothered, he decided to settle the question once and for all. He went to see Margaret, who was reposing at the home of her friend Dorothy Von Palmenberg, to confront her about the reporter's allegations.

"Why, yes," Margaret responded, "this Dr. Waite is the man with whom I have been studying in the Plaza in his studio."

"My only remark to her then was that it would be well for her to be a little more careful in choosing friends, as they might get her into trouble. Up to that time you called my attention to it I had not paid the slightest notice of the Peck case, or to Dr. Waite's connection with it."[80]

While Harry Mack Horton did his best to convince the world that his wife kept her clothes on during her afternoons with Waite at their Plaza suite, Arthur was moved to the alcoholics' ward of Bellevue Hospital, where he would stay until well enough to enter a suite at the city jail.[81]

"DOVE AMONG CROWS"

NEW YORK, NEW YORK

Saturday, March 25, 1916

Clara's mouth dropped open as she saw the Saturday, March 25 edition of the *Grand Rapids Herald*. The entire front page was devoted to Friday's revelations under the headline "'WOMAN OF MYSTERY' IN LIFE OF DR. WAITE TELLS STORY OF HER AFFAIR WITH DENTIST." The article detailed Waite's alleged tryst with Margaret Horton. Another item detailed Waite's partial confession.

Friends and family had kept the news from Clara out of fear that in her weakened state, she couldn't bear the shock. By Friday afternoon, they couldn't hide the news anymore.

Clara found herself drawn to a front-page item, featuring a close-up of Arthur's eyes, by *Herald* writer Marie Dille. In the article, Dille pondered Waite's hypnotic gaze and its effect on women. "They're the eyes that cause the feminine heart to flutter. They are compelling, irresistible, masterful and yet tender."

Clara clenched her teeth as she read the piece. "In the radius of their beams women forget to question the unreasonableness of the claims of the man accused of murder. All things are reasonable when accompanied by the flash of his glorious orbs. He won the world with the wonder of his smile and held it with his eyes."[82]

Another writer characterized Waite as a Jekyll and Hyde, not failing to recognize the similarities between the fictional character and the suspect. Like the fictional Dr. Henry Jekyll, Waite had two lives: the fantasy dental surgeon and the playboy; two wives, Clara and Margaret Horton; even two homes, the Coliseum and the Plaza.

Clara turned her attention to the article under the headline "Waite Attempts to Bribe Witness After Confession."

"How could he have done it? Arthur—I hate him. I want to see him punished," she hissed as she read about Waite's admissions to Swann in their Coliseum apartment. "He took from me my mother and my father, and they say he planned to kill me. I believe them. It is terrible."[83] She recoiled at the thought that she had just sent a message through the Waites professing her undying love and utter faith and devotion to Arthur.

Enraged, she threw down the newspaper. For a few minutes, she paced back and forth across the room but began to feel dizzy. She fell back on the bed and watched the ceiling spin. The shock overtaxed her, so she spent the rest of the day in bed.[84]

When she felt well enough to crawl out of bed later that afternoon, she decided she needed to do two things: she needed to once again change her will. If she had anything to say about it, Arthur Warren Waite had spent the last penny he would ever receive from the Pecks. She also needed to set the record straight. Reticent and humiliated, the good wife could stay mum no longer.

Dr. Wishart arrived at the Peck place, at Clara's request, around dinnertime. Clara greeted him, her face swollen and her eyes puffy. She had spent most of the afternoon sobbing. After offering Clara a few words of comfort, Wishart agreed to scribe a statement and send it to the press.

He sat at a writing desk, leaned over a sheet of paper and nodded.

Clara began:

> *I feel it my duty to the public to make the following statement. No previous statement said to have been made by me is authentic. I have given nothing whatever to the press.*[85]
>
> *When I was informed of the serious charges against my husband I was so shocked and amazed I could not believe them true. It seemed to me impossible that a man who had been so uniformly gentle and kind to me and apparently so loyal could be guilty of the crime with which he is charged.*
>
> *My faith in him began to be shaken when it was practically proved to me that Dr. Waite was living with another woman in the Plaza hotel.*
>
> *As the evidence against him increased from day to day I was compelled against my will and my deepest affection for him to accept the evidence as true.*
>
> *Of course I cannot and will not say he is guilty, but it certainly looks as if that is the fact.*

Clara Peck Waite in 1916. *From the Bain News Service, Library of Congress.*

I cannot lay bare my feelings to the world. No one knows except those who have suffered as I have what it means to have one's faith in a husband shattered and to be compelled to believe that in addition to disloyalty to me a great crime against my father and mother may have been committed.

As far as I am concerned, I must and will permit the law to take its course. I will stand aside and leave the whole matter to those who have the case in charge.

I cannot but pity a man who has apparently wasted his life and sacrificed everything that one should hold dear on the altar of selfishness.

I have told all I know frankly and fully to the authorities and will not discuss that statement, which is in their hands to view as they see fit.

It is all very sad and very terrible, all I ask is that I may be left alone with my friends to bear my sorrow the best I can.

Clara had already severed a part of herself from Arthur; she signed the note "CLARA LOUISE PECK," reverting to her maiden name.[86]

She gazed at the three-carat rock on her ring finger. Dr. Waite said the gemstone came from his South African diamond mine. Was it another lie? She slid the ring from her finger and laid it on the bedroom nightstand.

By Saturday morning, Swann had become convinced that Arthur Warren Waite had attempted to kill his in-laws by infecting them with dangerous bacilli. When the germs didn't kill the Pecks as planned, Waite turned to the more reliable poison, arsenic.[87]

With the case against Waite airtight, Swann turned his attention to anyone who might have known something about the crime or coverup and might help him further strengthen his case. One name topped his list: Margaret Horton.

Swann told reporters on Friday night that he had no knowledge Waite had any accomplices, and he emphasized that mere knowledge of criminal intent didn't make a person an accomplice. Nonetheless, Margaret Horton became a target in his investigation.[88]

To reporters, it seemed as though the DA was trying too hard to convince them he had no other suspects in the crime. Naturally, they became convinced he had, and thus newspaper reporters eyed Margaret Horton with even more suspicion than before.

There was plenty of material to keep reporters gossiping. When Margaret's identity as "Mrs. A.W. Walters" became known, Swann had asked Harry

Mack Horton to provide a photograph of his wife. Horton sent two snapshots. On the back of one photo, Swann immediately recognized the name of Dr. Muller—the physician who helped Waite acquire arsenic to "kill cats." Waite, Swann had learned, also expressed his interest in bacteriology to Dr. Muller and asked him for an introduction to an expert in the field.

Scrawled onto the back of the other photograph were the name and telephone number of Grace Hoffman, a professional singer. On Saturday morning, Swann had an interesting chat with the pretty, petite vocalist. She relayed two conversations she had had with Margaret Horton that caused the DA to sit up in his chair. A few days before Aunt Catherine gave Waite $40,000, Margaret boasted that she had just come into a considerable amount of money. A few days after John Peck died, Margaret said she was in deep trouble, although she didn't specify what type of trouble. Swann also learned that when Waite purchased specimens of typhoid and diphtheria, he was with an unidentified female.

Margaret Horton had some explaining to do, so Swann invited her in for an interview with John Dooling and George Brothers.

<hr>

While Waite's "studio companion" waited in the hallway of the criminal courts building along with her lawyer, Harold Spielberg, Dooling questioned one of the men who supplied Waite with dozens of germ cultures.

William Webber rubbed his hands together as Dooling stared at him. The documents found in Waite's safety deposit box led straight to Webber, a clerk at Cornell Medical School's bacteriology laboratory.

On six different occasions, the frightened clerk said, Waite came to the laboratory to acquire specimens. Webber admitted procuring the bacilli, including typhoid, pneumonia, diphtheria and tuberculosis, but he insisted he played no part in any murder plot.

"He asked for the germs and represented himself to be a practicing physician and surgeon and told me he was conducting a series of experiments with cats," Webber explained. Waite told the clerk that he brought the germs home, where he conducted his experimentations.

Dooling immediately recognized the reference to cats—the same reference Waite used when he obtained arsenic from Timmerman's pharmacy.

Webber scratched his head. Waite, he added, always dropped by after hours. "It was irregular to give him the germs after hours, but I believed what he said and let him have them."[89]

The "dove among crows," Mrs. Margaret Weaver Horton. This is one of three photographs that circulated widely in newspapers throughout the United States. *From the* New York World-Telegram *and the* Sun Newspaper *Photograph Collection, Library of Congress.*

Webber said that Waite acquired the specimens during the period from December 22 until March 8—a timeline that led investigators to believe that Waite tried to infect John Peck but became impatient when it didn't work and turned to arsenic instead. The receipt proving Waite purchased the poison from Timmerman was dated March 9.

Webber also said that a woman accompanied Waite on one occasion.

Dooling called Margaret Horton in from the hallway.

"That's the woman," Webber exclaimed. "She came with Dr. Waite when he bought the germ cultures."

It was Margaret Horton's turn on the hot seat. She and her attorney took their places in the wooden armchairs while Dooling and Brothers whispered to each other. For "Mrs. A.W. Walters," it would be the beginning of a very long day. Over the next six hours, the assistant district attorneys grilled Margaret Horton.[90]

Their first question: was she "K. Adams"?

Margaret crinkled up her nose. She had no idea who that person was. She did, however, admit fibbing to reporters when she denied knowing Waite checked her into the Plaza as "Mrs. Walters."[91]

She denied any knowledge of Waite's plot to murder the Peck family. Waite always spoke about his in-laws, she explained, with affection and praise. He never alluded to their demise or any plot, although he did remark about their poor health on numerous occasions.

Waite, Margaret said, told her he was studying bacteriology and even took her to a laboratory where he acquired specimens. Waite told her these were chemicals he was using to test their effect on various bacteria. Waite even showed her the germs under a microscope. "Why, he put some of them under a microscope and let me see them wiggle."

Next, Dooling asked Margaret to detail the nature of her relationship with Waite.

She insisted that they never slept together, describing their relationship as platonic. They playacted, that was all. "We studied Shakespeare. Dr. Waite played Romeo to my Juliet," Margaret said.[92]

Margaret remained calm as the district attorney hurled one accusation after another at her, but she grew enraged when Brothers suggested that Waite paid her for her affection.

The allegation stemmed from a curious coincidence: the same day that Catherine Peck's attorney raised $8,000 from a real estate transaction, Harry Mack Horton and his wife obtained about the same amount.

This sudden incursion of money coupled with Horton's seemingly laissez faire attitude toward Margaret's playacting with another man led

Dooling and Brothers to suggest a scenario in which Waite paid her for her favors.

Margaret offered an alternate explanation for the large sum of money. "He [Harry Mack Horton] got the money from wireless telegraphy with Mexico. He didn't get it all at once, but in small sums." She felt her temperature rise and her heart beating in her neck. She hated it when they besmirched Harry. Just because he stood by her, investigators and press alike had dragged out every detail of his life in some perverted effort to make him seem like a criminal. They even brought up the fact that he filed for bankruptcy on January 1, 1915, only to be discharged on December 29, 1915, as if it suggested something nefarious. It was true that she first met Waite around the time Harry was discharged from bankruptcy, but that was nothing more than coincidental.

She paused and drew in a deep breath to calm her nerves before continuing. "I've only done what a million other women do constantly, in being guilty of a slight indiscretion. It was just my luck to have it all come out like this." She addressed the allegation that she had planned to run off with Waite, explaining that she studied languages for her stage career and for no other reason. "Of course, it didn't imply that I was going abroad with Dr. Waite because I studied the languages with him. I couldn't sing Italian operas in English, could I?"[93]

Margaret denied ever singing in a disreputable establishment. She hated the description "cabaret singer" that was used by several reporters. She considered it an insult. "I was never a cabaret singer," she insisted, defensively. "I never sang in any hotel except the Metropole and that was only for the opening week, but I sang at entertainments and concerts, because I was then studying at the Cincinnati College of Music and needed the money, as I was supporting myself and paying for my musical education."[94]

Arthur, she explained, never gave her anything, although he did pay for her lessons at the YMCA School of Expression.

Dooling asked her about the diamond ring Waite gave her when he said goodbye.

Here, Spielberg spoke on Margaret's behalf. She did receive the ring, "but she gave it back. It [the ring] cost $2,000, but she gave it back."[95]

Margaret blushed and hoped that Harry didn't recognize her embarrassment. She wanted that ring, so badly in fact, that she would later attempt to get it back through Spielberg.

The press had a field day following Margaret Horton's interview. The headlines transformed her into a wild, home-wrecking seductress with a history of domestic destruction.

A *Grand Rapids News* writer mocked Margaret and alluded to an undercover relationship when he wrote that she and Waite "studied Romeo and Juliet in a very realistic manner."[96]

The dailies of both Grand Rapids and New York aired the dirty laundry of Cincinnati engineer Paul Held, who told reporters that Margaret Horton destroyed his marriage, although not in the way most would expect. When "Otila" came to live with him and his wife, Held explained, his wife fell "completely under her control."

"Men flocked to see Otila," Held said, describing Margaret's magnetic charm. "Finally, my wife began to love Otila more than she did me. She sued me for divorce and named Otila in the petition. The girl skipped out before the case was tried, but my wife got the divorce. Otila came back and lived with my wife for a year and a half."[97]

Ray Schindler, always one step ahead of Swann's men, realized that the evidence of Waite's diabolical plot to infect the Pecks would be found in the Coliseum.

That afternoon, while Dooling and Brothers interrogated Margaret Horton, Schindler and Andrew Taylor made a sweep of Waite's apartment to search for any possible evidence missed during earlier searches. They emptied bookcases, pulled out dresser drawers and overturned cabinets.

They placed on the kitchen table anything and everything related to the biological warfare Waite apparently waged against the Pecks.

Their two-hour sweep netted a large cache of evidence. Stacks of glass slides piled in tiers on the table glittered under the sunlight. In all, they found 180 slides with labels such as "tetanus," "Asiatic cholera," "typhus," "pneumonia" and "tuberculosis."

By Saturday evening, March 25, Margaret Horton's face had appeared on front pages across the nation. Thanks to the *Evening World*, she had gained national infamy as Waite's other woman despite her insistence that they weren't lovers. Harry Mack Horton became the unwitting victim of Margaret's newfound stardom. Margaret loved Harry, so she wanted to do everything she could to protect her image and that of her husband. After her six-hour marathon interrogation, she gave a brief statement to the press.

Margaret wanted to emphasize that she and Waite knew about, even spoke about, each other's spouses. "As I told you last night, he often spoke to me about his wife, and about his father-in-law. He wanted me to come up to his house to meet his wife. She would just fall in love with you, and so would Father, he told me. I would willingly have gone to visit his people, but it just seemed as if my many engagements would never give me the opportunity. On the other hand, as I told, I was just as urgent in asking him to come to the house and meet Mr. Horton."

As for her role as "Mrs. Walters," Margaret explained, "I told you last night the circumstances under which we engaged the room at the Plaza and just what my position was there in regard to him."

A few of the reporters chuckled at Margaret's choice of words. Over the past few days, many of them wondered about the positions she and Dr. Waite had shared at the Plaza.

Margaret went on to explain why she made such a hasty retreat from the hotel. When Waite returned to Grand Rapids after delivering the body of John Peck, she said, he called her at the Plaza. She heard an uncharacteristic nervousness in his tone when he told her to leave immediately. "They are accusing me of something I didn't do. You must leave at once," he said.

She did as she was told and promptly paid the bill of $250, which raised a few eyebrows, because Margaret insisted she didn't know that Waite had dubbed her "Mrs. A.W. Walters." If she paid the bill for the room, the reporters wondered, she must have known about the pseudonyms Waite chose. They also quoted the Plaza's assistant manager who stated that Waite, who presented himself as "Mr. Walters," actually introduced Margaret as his wife.[98]

Few readers believed that Margaret Horton's sheets at the Plaza were white, and even fewer understood Harry's unrelenting loyalty—a fact Harry discovered when they returned home that evening to find a mailbox stuffed with letters.

"Open your eyes, you boob!" screamed one letter.

The negative press caused Horton to go on the offensive. In a lengthy interview, he characterized Margaret as a "dove among crows" in New York City. People simply didn't understand Margaret's innocent nature, he said.

"How do you know your wife is a spotless dove?" the reporter asked.

"Well, I'll tell you. In the first place, I know my wife is a beautiful woman. But that is no reason why I should watch her as a hawk does a dove. She is armored by her innocence. And I am not afraid of other men, male crows, for I treat women with chivalry, and I expect that other men will do the same."[99]

While Harry Mack Horton described his Shangri-La, one of the city's crows was trying to figure a way out of its cage.

Waite couldn't afford Stanchfield, and his family, resigned to Arthur's guilt, decided they would attempt to keep him out of the electric chair by plea bargaining with Swann for a reduced charge of second-degree murder.

The family agreed that their appeal to Swann would depend on several factors: a complete confession of guilt, evidence that Arthur was mentally unbalanced, cooperation from the Peck family and consent from Catherine Peck to pay for the attorney. Together, they could only muster $5,000, but perhaps, with mercy, Catherine Peck would do this one last thing to keep Arthur out of the chair.

Walter Drew, Catherine Peck's attorney, circa 1916. *From the Bain News Service, Library of Congress.*

Distraught and emotional, Frank Waite asked Catherine Peck's attorney, Walter Drew, to represent Arthur in the proceedings. A reporter eavesdropped on the pathetic sight.

"Mr. Drew," Frank Waite wailed, "for God's sake, help us. We know Arthur is guilty, but help us save the boy from the electric chair. Help us to do that and we ask no more."[100] The reporter scribbled Waite's words in a notebook while Drew contemplated the proposal. Frank shrugged, "It is hopeless to present that Arthur is not guilty."

Drew, realizing the conflict of interest, said he couldn't defend Arthur but agreed to help find a suitable representative. He phoned Catherine Peck, who agreed to try to dissuade her family from pushing for the death penalty.

Nonetheless, Drew doubted an insanity plea would succeed. Swann indicated that he had obtained enough evidence to quash such a defense. Besides, the Waite family couldn't afford the high cost of hiring alienists to testify on Waite's behalf.

Meanwhile, Frank went to Bellevue, where he would try talking Arthur into giving a full confession.

8

"THE MAN FROM EGYPT"

NEW YORK, NEW YORK

Tuesday, March 28–Wednesday, March 29, 1916

Ray Schindler stood in a corner of the room as Frank Waite approached his brother's bedside. He eavesdropped as Frank explained that Swann might entertain a plea deal keeping Arthur off death row if Arthur gave a complete confession.

Arthur stared at Frank for a few seconds, shrugged and agreed to tell the truth. Tears welled up at the corners of his eyes and began sliding down his cheeks as he made several admissions. He had lied about obtaining arsenic for Peck's suicide. He bought the poison specifically to do away with his father-in-law. When he could no longer stand the old man's suffering, he finished him off with a chloroform rag and a pillow he pressed against Peck's face. At first, Waite denied murdering Hannah Peck but then changed his story and admitted spiking her food with bacteria cultures.[101]

Frank Waite grasped his brother's hand and gave it a gentle squeeze.

For the first time, Frank felt a sense of hope. He would broker a deal with the DA. If Arthur agreed to repeat his confession to Swann, he might not have to die in Sing Sing's electric chair. Arthur agreed, once again and for a stenographer, to detail every facet of the twisted fairy tale he had authored for the Peck family.

Frank also wanted to do what he could to return the money Arthur had taken. He asked Arthur to sign a document that turned over his assets to Catherine Peck. Without question, Arthur scribbled his name at the bottom of the paper.

Frank then left the ward and called Swann to tell him about the confession. Swann arranged for a transcriptionist to accompany him to Bellevue the next morning.

———⇒•⇐———

That evening, a stunning twist occurred in the case. Walter Deuel, the attorney who had consulted with the Peck family, decided to represent Arthur Warren Waite.

He took the case, he explained to the press, at the request of Catherine Peck, to make sure his client received a fair shake. "I assure you," Deuel stated, "that I am retained only to see that full justice is done. I am sure the district attorney wants only to bring out all the facts."[102] Deuel, the former head of the DA's "homicide bureau," knew his business.

———⇒•⇐———

Swann, followed by a transcriptionist, Mancuso, Dooling, Brothers and Schindler, shuffled into Waite's Bellevue room, expecting to hear the climactic confession Frank Waite had promised. It would conclude one of the most fascinating criminal cases in the city's history.

Schindler thought Waite looked like a man about to spill his guts. He had seen that same agonizing look on the faces of many suspects. But each time Waite began to say something remotely incriminating, Deuel interrupted and said that his client was far too exhausted to continue.

Deuel, however, failed to completely muzzle his client, who shocked everyone when he remembered a pertinent detail he had neglected to tell Swann in his first confession: the "man from Egypt."[103]

His body, Waite explained, contained two souls who lived side by side: one gentle and kind and the other malevolent. "Another man, or spirit, at times occupies my body and makes me two personalities—one good and the other bad. I was powerless against him. When I felt him take hold of me I knew I was gone."

Brothers and Swann exchanged a quick glance. Waite, it appeared, had fallen into a fantasy world as an attempt to preempt the insanity defense both knew they would confront in court. The story sounded familiar to Brothers, who remembered reading about the strange case of George W. Wood, who murdered a shopkeeper named George Williams in 1905. After his capture, Wood claimed to be possessed by a double he called "the little black man" who moved him to murder.[104]

Frank's heart sank. He shielded his face with the palm of his hand as he watched Arthur talk his way out of any possible plea bargain. Deuel stared at Waite, dumbfounded.

"Doctor," Swann asked, "can't you tell us where this man or spirit comes from?"

"No, I can't judge."

"But, doctor, this man has been with you so much and you have talked with him so much, can't you give us any idea where he comes from?"

"It must be from Egypt. Yes, sir, it's an Egyptian spirit, for he's always talking about Egypt and Egyptian things."

Dooling jumped in. "You mean Egypt, Missouri, don't you?"

"No, I mean Egypt, Africa."[105]

Swann didn't know what to say. He had seen other suspects feign insanity, but Waite's fiction seemed so bizarre, so far-fetched, he wanted to laugh. Then he glanced at Frank Waite and remembered how Arthur's bedside confession had emotionally unhinged him. All of a sudden, it seemed more pathetic than humorous. Schindler, though, cracked a smile. Brothers wondered what Margaret Horton would say if she knew that her acting sessions with Waite would culminate in this, the performance of Waite's life.

Waite admitted, without even a smirk on his face, "it was with me when I procured the germs that I administered to Mrs. Peck. It was not I who killed my mother-in-law, but the bad part of me—this Egyptian spirit who killed her, through me." The bad man, he said, also made him kill his father-in-law.

"He did it," Waite explained without a hint of emotion in his voice. "The bad man, the man from Egypt. I was afraid of him. He made me do terrible things. Sometimes when I felt him after me I would run away. I ran into the park once and tried to get away from him there, but he caught me. I told Clara about it. It was only last night the good man came back."

"Now tell me, doctor, did you have any accomplices?"

"Only Kane, who embalmed Mr. Peck's body, and of course that bad man from Egypt inside me whom I was unable to control." Waite explained that when he returned to New York from Grand Rapids, the evil entity inhabited his body. So when he tried to pay off Kane, it was the bad man making him do it.

Swann frowned as the possible implications of a crooked embalmer hit him. He asked Waite to describe the bribe.

Waite said that when he returned to the Coliseum after arriving from Grand Rapids, he found John Potter waiting at his door. The undertaker had come to collect payment for the embalming of John Peck's body.

Potter, according to Waite, had heard that the district attorney wanted a sample of the embalming fluid, so Waite said it would be best if it contained arsenic. Potter then suggested Waite pay Kane to lie about the contents of his embalming fluid and prepare a doctored sample for the DA. "That would cost money," Potter suggested. When Waite asked how much, Potter said he didn't know for sure but added, "You cannot expect Kane to do this and put himself in that position without being paid well for it." Potter, Waite said, also suggested he pay off pharmacist Richard Timmerman, from whom he had purchased the arsenic that wound up in John Peck's soup.

Following Potter's advice, Waite wrote out a check for $9,400, dated March 20 and drawn on the Corn Exchange Bank, and handed it to Kane. Dooling nodded. This explained Waite's sale of one hundred shares from Catherine Peck's stock portfolio. Realizing over $9,000, he deposited the money in an account only to subsequently withdraw it. "After I handed Kane this check," Waite continued, "he went out, but came back shortly and said Potter had advised him not to bank it and Kane asked for the money in cash."

At this point, Waite explained, he suspected the police might have tapped his telephone, so he jotted Potter a note. "Don't telephone me, and don't let Kane telephone me, for the wires are tapped. Don't worry about the check." Then, acquiescing to their demand for cash, he wrote out a second check for the amount of $9,000 and asked a garage owner named Cimiotti to cash it for him. Later that morning, he met Kane at a cigar store and gave him a wad of banknotes in denominations of $500s, $100s and $50s. Kane, Waite said, also kept the $9,400 check because he believed Waite intended to pay him as much as $25,000.

Later, Waite asked Kane, "Did you get the arsenic?"

"Yes," Waite said he replied, "I went way down on Long Island and got three sticks of arsenic from a gardener I have known for years."

But Waite never heard of "sticks of arsenic." "I pulled down the books in my laboratory and began studying the subject of arsenic with reference to gardening."

Swann smiled. Waite's tale provided a convenient explanation for the medical references containing bookmarks in pages discussing arsenic.

The district attorney's smile disappeared when Waite alleged that Kane told him he had falsified samples before and boasted of helping others evade convictions by fabricating evidence. Potter had helped embalm the body of William Marsh, for whose murder Albert Patrick was convicted but later pardoned. Kane did the embalming work on Katherine J. Adams—the victim who inspired the "K. Adams" pseudonym. Waite's story, if true, raised doubts about tainted evidence in those cases.

On the other hand, Swann knew Waite was a habitual liar. Nonetheless, the DA began to envision a scenario in which either Potter or Kane sent the "K. Adams" telegram as a way to blackmail or coerce hush money from Waite. He immediately dispatched Cunniff to the undertaker's establishment with a subpoena in hand. He also ordered the arrest of Eugene Oliver Kane.[106]

Swann left Bellevue after half an hour, deeply disturbed. He didn't have the coup de grace of a full confession, and Waite had added another element to an already convoluted case when he accused the undertakers.

A group of reporters spotted Swann coming out of the hospital and asked him about the confession. He gave a brief statement.

"Dr. Waite made no confession. No, he did not even admit he had killed Mr. Peck," he told the reporters. "[He] did not admit murder of any kind."

"But," one stunned reporter asked, "I thought you came up, judge, with the understanding that he was prepared to make a full confession."

"It seems that Dr. Waite was fully prepared to make a full confession to me, but that his counsel would not let him."[107]

Others on Swann's staff, however, believed that Deuel had pulled a fast one on the DA. He had planned all along for Swann to hear the "man from Egypt" story as a prelude to an insanity defense.

Swann declared that he would reject any insanity plea attempted by Waite's counsel. If Waite was insane, he would have to prove it in court. And, Swann noted, he would follow the wishes of Percy Peck and seek the death penalty.

Waite's act didn't fool anyone. A *New York Tribune* writer sarcastically described the situation: "There being no psychic Ellis Island, the man from Egypt came to this country, heaven only knows when. He entered into Dr. Waite long ago, evicting the soul the man had been equipped with at birth, and reigning at intervals in that spirit's stead."[108]

⇒•●•⇐

Waite's "man from Egypt" story created a problem for Walter Rogers Deuel, who wanted to stage a legitimate insanity defense. He bought a train ticket to Grand Rapids, where he hoped to interview Waite's family members about a possible strain of mental instability running back through generations.

That evening, just before he climbed aboard a westbound train, Deuel outlined his strategy to the press: "Until I can have the advice of medical authorities, I think it best for Dr. Waite to be kept as quiet as possible. I wish, however, to deny positively that our defense will be based on any such ridiculous stuff as 'the evil spirit from Egypt,' which the papers described with such detail this morning."

Deuel, forced to do some spin control, offered an alternate explanation for Waite's bizarre tale. "Dr. Waite never said seriously he was possessed of an evil man from Egypt. He never has pretended that he had hallucinations. What he did say was there was a 'bad side to him, and a good side,' and that sometimes this bad side which he described as 'he' got the better of him. Then along comes the district attorney. One of his assistants got rough. He said to Dr. Waite, 'who the hell is he, who is this accomplice?' Dr. Waite resented his manner, and becoming sarcastic, finally said he didn't know who he was, but presumed 'he' came from Egypt. That was literally all there was to it. Dr. Waite simply joked with the district attorney's office, and they took it all seriously."[109]

⟞•◦•⟝

Clara, like Deuel, saw right through Waite's ruse. As she read the news item quoting Waite, she reread one line over and over: "I told Clara about it." Enraged, she tossed the newspaper aside and telephoned Reverend Wishart. She wanted to call Arthur's bluff, but she didn't want to face the press just yet.

A few minutes later, Wishart arrived at the Peck mansion to once again scribe a statement.

Wishart wrote while Clara talked from her bedside. When she finished, he handed her the transcript. Clara read it over, managed a faint smile and handed it back to Wishart.

From the Peck estate, Wishart made a beeline to the nearest Western Union office and wired the message to the *New York Herald*.

"He said no word to me about such a condition. This evil personality has been conjured up since his arrest, and the man from Egypt is a rank myth. This is Arthur's attempt to free himself, but I will never help him in it. He murdered my mother. I know he did it intentionally. He had planned it all and he made his plans when he was in possession of every faculty."[110]

⟞•◦•⟝

On Wednesday afternoon, March 29, Cunniff dragged the stunned, forty-five-year-old undertaker John S. Potter into Swann's office for what turned out to be a long night of interrogation.

Potter, frightened, adamantly denied writing the "K. Adams" telegram or playing any role whatsoever in an extortion scheme.

He did admit to warning Waite about the investigation afoot and receiving the letter in which Waite commanded him not to telephone because his line was tapped, but when Swann asked him why Waite would send such a letter, he couldn't produce an answer.

After Potter left Swann's office, Swann received word that the grand jury was ready to indict Waite for the murder of John Peck. But after speaking with Waite, Swann suspected Kane of possibly extorting hush money from Waite. He decided to withhold the indictment until he spoke with the undertaker.

Swann had dispatched a team of detectives to find Kane, but despite turning the city upside down, they still could not find him.

⟶•◦•⟵

While Swann grilled Potter at the Criminal Courts Building, the Peck family held a conference at Aunt Catherine's Park Avenue Hotel room.

Percy Peck, legs crossed, leafed through the stack of newspapers that Walter Drew had collected. He nodded as he read through the coverage. It was mostly accurate, but in a few instances, imaginative journalists had predictably sensationalized an already-sensational case.

In the days since the case broke, newspapermen had aired several baseless rumors, and Waite became a larger-than-life villain. One that made the rounds was the rumor that Waite planned to murder both Margaret and her husband. This allegation persisted despite Margaret's insistence that it was based on an error. When a reporter suggested Waite may have wanted to poison her, she facetiously replied, "Did he?" The reporter either didn't catch Margaret Horton's sarcasm or ignored it entirely, and Margaret became yet another one of Waite's intended victims.[111]

Waite, the rumor mill also suggested, used his tennis chums as guinea pigs for germ experimentation. According to reports, assistant district attorneys uncovered evidence that several friends became ill after spending time with Waite. Swann, however, condemned this story as a myth.

Coselia Corbitt, a Grand Rapids native studying music in New York and a close friend of Clara Peck, supposedly wrote a letter home containing a damaging piece of hearsay. "I'll soon be spending the Peck millions," she said she heard Waite remark. But when Swann's men cornered Corbitt, she denied ever hearing such a statement or writing such a letter.

The Peck family, likewise, became victims of the rumormongering. In ink, Percy appeared as a revenge-driven snob and Aunt Catherine a guileless woman so duped by Waite that she would go so far as to fund his defense. Percy glanced over at Aunt Catherine. She looked bewildered, her hands shaking slightly.

They agreed that they would play no part in Waite's defense. Aware of the press indicating Aunt Catherine's desire to pay for Waite's legal fees, they issued a formal statement through Walter Drew.

They wanted to dispel several rumors:

Percy Peck was not motivated by revenge;

No member of the Peck family arranged for Walter Deuel to take the case;

Catherine Peck did not offer to bankroll Arthur's defense.

The brief statement was signed by Percy S. Peck, Mrs. Clara Peck Waite, Catherine A. Peck and Mrs. Percy Peck.[112]

9

RAISING KANE

NEW YORK, NEW YORK
Thursday, March 30–Friday, March 31, 1916

Swann glared as Eugene Oliver Kane walked into his office alongside his lawyer on the afternoon of March 30. He had decided to surrender himself to authorities.

The terrified undertaker was ready to talk in exchange for a promise that he would not face any criminal charges. Reluctantly, Swann agreed, *if* Kane told the truth about his dealings with Waite.

The first question: did Kane send the "K. Adams" telegram? Like Potter, Kane denied having anything to do with it.

Kane described his embalming of John Peck and insisted he had followed the law to a T. "I used the same fluid I have been using for the last seven years. It is made of formaldehyde, glycerin and soda phosphates. There was no arsenic in it. I never use arsenic."

That part of Kane's story, Swann realized, was true; a sample of his embalming fluid did not contain arsenic.

Swann asked Kane to describe Waite's attempted bribe.

Kane gave a scene-by-scene description of his meetings with Waite on March 19–20. When Waite asked, "Could arsenic be put in the embalming fluid?" Kane replied, "It could, but I wouldn't do it because it was against the law." When they met the next morning, Kane said, Waite shoved "a large roll of something"—he didn't know what at the time—in his pocket and disappeared. Later he discovered what his pocket contained.

"When I got home I opened the roll and saw $50 bills and $100 bills and two $500s. There was so much money I got afraid and never counted it."

He became nervy, he said, and decided to bury the money. "About a week later, I took this roll of money down to Greenport, Long Island, and went down to the shore, and there, I wrapped the money in a piece of paper and put it into a marshmallow can and wrapped that in a piece of paper and buried it in the sand."[113]

Swann stared at Kane, who puckered his lips and shrugged.

Swann faced a dilemma with Kane. For the most part, the bones of his story—where he met Waite and when—matched those of Potter and Waite. The devil was in the details. Waite made it sound like Potter and Kane willingly conspired to provide false testimony and even possibly doctor evidence. Then again, Waite could lie with the best of them. But, Swann had discovered, Kane was no angel, either. He had done time for bigamy.

Who was he to believe, Waite or Kane? Either of their scenarios fit the known facts.

Swann smiled as he remembered a line from a Sherlock Holmes story: "There is nothing more deceptive than an obvious fact."[114]

Perhaps a sand dune on Long Island contained the clue that would separate fact from fiction.

⸺⊷◆⊶⸺

On Friday morning, March 31, an icy spring wind swept across the sandy beach at Orient Point—the tip of Long Island where Kane said he buried Waite's $9,000 bribe. Kane led John Cunniff and Ansell Young, the manager of the Orient Point Hotel, through the sand dunes toward the spot where he had buried the tin can containing Waite's bankroll.

It was a weird episode, Cunniff thought as he followed Kane. The shady undertaker would not tell Swann where he buried the stash but agreed to lead a detective to the exact spot on Long Island where, guilt ridden and afraid, he had buried it a week earlier.

Their odd odyssey began at eight o'clock on the morning of March 31, when Kane met Cunniff at the Long Island Railroad Station and ordered him to buy two tickets to Greenport. Cunniff rented a car, and for two miles, they sped along the beach road until the car became stuck in a deep drift of sand. They hiked back to Greenport, where Cunniff chartered a boat.

For a second time, Kane and Cunniff set out for Orient Point, but after a few minutes, Cunniff realized that the motorboat didn't have a rudder. It took about an hour to paddle back to shore, where they came across Ansell Young.

Young recognized Kane, who was a frequent visitor to his hotel. After a brief chat, Young agreed to help. For a third time, Kane and Cunniff, this time with Ansell Young as their pilot, headed for Orient Point. They traveled for about five miles to East Marion Landing and went ashore. They hiked another mile until they came to a tall tree with three branches that pointed north, east and west.

By the time they reached the tree, it was high noon, and John Cunniff had reached the end of his rope.

Kane knelt down and felt through the tall sea grass for a rusty tin can he used to mark the spot. When he found it, he tossed it aside and jabbed his pocketknife into the ground. The knife struck something solid, and Kane dropped to his knees and began scooping out handfuls of dirt. A few minutes later, he pulled a tin can from the hole and handed it to Cunniff.

Cunniff pried back the lid, reached inside the can and removed a small package wrapped with brown paper. He gently tugged at the paper, and it came away, revealing a roll of banknotes with a $500 bill on the outside. They had just unearthed a portion of the money Catherine Peck had entrusted to Waite and solid evidence of an attempted bribe. The other portion of the bribe—the uncashed $9,400 check—remained missing.

With Young and Kane watching, Cunniff sat down and counted the money. The roll contained exactly $7,800—$1,200 shy of the bribe Kane said Waite paid him. Cunniff repeated the count three times, and each time he arrived at the same figure.

Cunniff stared at Kane for a few seconds. "My man, you're shy," he said with a wry smile.

Kane shrugged. "How do I know it's shy? I told you and the judge [Swann] that I never counted the roll the doctor gave me. I was too nervous."

"Well," Cunniff remarked sarcastically, "it's gone anyhow. Maybe the man from Egypt came and took his rakeoff."[115]

Young chuckled; Kane wiped the beads of sweat from his forehead.

———※·◦·※———

While Kane led the treasure hunt on Long Island, Walter Deuel traveled to Grand Rapids, where he gathered information about history of insanity in the Waite family

Deuel interviewed Waite's family and friends and found evidence of insanity running throughout the Jackson branch of the Waite family tree. He discovered that Arthur's grandfather Milo left home one day never to return, and two of his father's cousins spent time in insane asylums.

When he returned to his New York office, Deuel learned that the grand jury had reached a decision. They had returned an indictment against Waite for two counts: the first charged Waite with using arsenic to murder John Peck, and the second charged him with using "a certain deadly poison, to the said grand jury likewise unknown."[116] The second charge referred to the possibility that Waite had murdered Peck with a deadly bacteria or virus.

Deuel carried the news to Bellevue, where he found Warren and Sarah Waite flanking their son's bed. Arthur was unmoved by the indictment. "It's just as I expected," he said flatly.

When Deuel said Waite would likely face the death penalty, Sarah Waite began to sob. "My son! My son!" she shrieked. "My poor son!"

Warren threw his arms around his wife in a vain attempt to calm her and escorted her out of the room.

Once Sarah Waite was out of earshot, Deuel suggested an insanity defense. Waite glared at his lawyer. "I am just as sane as you are. You can't help me in that way," he snapped. "I'm not afraid of the electric chair."[117]

⊰⊷●⊷⊱

By March 31, Catherine, Percy and Clara had all condemned Waite in a public statement. Even Waite's mother declared he must not have been himself when he poisoned his father-in-law. Margaret Horton, however, stood by her other man when she spoke to a reporter.

"I would stake my life on my conviction that he never planned to kill anybody," Margaret told a shocked journalist. "It was not in him to do harm to anybody. He would not kill a fly."

"Do you believe that Waite has made the confessions attributed to him?"

"I do not. Either those supposed confessions were made out of whole cloth, or Dr. Waite was drugged and did not know what he was saying."

"What would you say if Dr. Waite should tell you now that he had committed these crimes?"

"I should believe he was drugged."

"What would you think if he should state under oath that he was guilty?"

"Then I should believe he was insane, and I should devote all my resources to proving him insane."[118]

When the reporter left, Margaret took out a sheet of perfumed writing paper, dipped her fountain pen in the ink well and began: "Dear Doctor, I am oh, so sorry for you. I know you are absolutely innocent. Be brave and strong. I shall come to see you to-morrow."[119]

Tomorrow, however, would never come. Swann refused to allow Margaret Horton access to Waite. So "Mr. and Mrs. A.W. Walters" began penning each other letters.[120]

Neither of them realized that these letters would later provide Swann with a damaging piece of evidence.

※◆※

Walter Deuel slapped the Monday, April 3 edition of the *Sun* on his desk. He ran his finger across the page as he read the article "DR. WAITE INSISTS THAT HE IS SANE." The article was a follow-up to the previous day's front-page item. On Sunday, April 2, New Yorkers read all about a curious letter Waite sent, through Deuel, to an editor at the *World*. It contained Waite's latest admission of guilt, this time without the "man from Egypt." This was the fourth time—following the partial confession to Swann, the confession to Frank Waite and the "man from Egypt" tale—that Waite admitted to having a hand in the death of John Peck.

> *I have been informed that I have been indicted for the crime of murder in the first degree.*
> *I know the punishment is death.*
> *The indictment is just and the penalty is one that I deserve, for I have killed. I killed John E. Peck and his wife.*
> *The* World *has always been a fair and impartial paper and one that has always tried to get the facts for the public, and I find that in my case you have searched for the facts and have given them to the public, and therefore in making this my only statement to the public, which I feel in duty bound to make, I address myself to you.*
> *I have thought and thought and thought while lying in my bed here in the hospital. I have gone over all the incidents of the last few months and my life and I have made my peace with my Creator. I now desire to make atonement for the wrong I have done.*
> *It is a terrible grief to me that I should have brought such obloquy and shame upon my wife and upon the name of my good parents and made my brothers suffer as they do.*
> *I am relieved to make this, my confession.*
> *Signed, Arthur Warren Waite*[121]

After signing the letter, Waite, apparently struggling with a guilty conscience, summoned Deuel to his bedside and made another statement.

In a rambling narrative, Waite detailed his plot to poison the Pecks, including his intention to murder Clara, and explained that it emanated from his desire to obtain easy money. He explained that he didn't include this aspect of his plot in his letter to the *World* because he wanted to limit his latest confession to the crimes he had actually committed. He said he didn't fear death. In fact, he welcomed it and expressed his desire to go to the chair.

He also addressed his sanity. "There is no use to try to make it appear that I am insane," Waite said. "I'm perfectly sane. My mind is as clear as a bell, and I think in straight lines. That 'bad man from Egypt' story is sheer nonsense. It developed from my trying to joke with a most serious-minded assistant district attorney, Dooling. I don't want an insanity defense offered. I shall state in court that I'm not crazy and never have been."

Waite asked Deuel to relay his statement to the press, which the lawyer did in a telephone call to the *World*. The next day—April 3—the confession, and Waite's follow-up statement, hit the newsstands.

Deuel's lips curled up in a half smile as he reread Waite's statement about sanity. He hoped that Waite's frank admission of guilt would lead others to conclude that only an insane man would act that way.

10

A QUESTION OF MIND

NEW YORK, NEW YORK

Tuesday, April 4–Monday, May 15, 1916

Arthur Warren Waite had, a *Sun* reporter wrote, left "fingerprints of indiscretion" all over the city.[122]

Harry Mack Horton's "dove among crows" analogy and Margaret's countless reiterations of her platonic-only relationship with Waite could not explain why detectives found Arthur's lavender pajamas—a gift from Clara—in their Plaza studio. Waite even decorated the love nest with art from the Coliseum apartment.

On April 4, Clara filed for a divorce, citing Arthur's "open and notorious adultery with one Mrs. Margaret Horton" and "persons unknown to the plaintiff" as one factor. The bill of complaint also alleged that Waite, after poisoning Clara's parents, would have made an attempt on her life. "From the result of investigation," Clara stated in the complaint, "your oratrix verily believes it to be true that the defendant actually had in mind to poison various other members of her family and indeed had especially in mind to poison your oratrix."[123]

———————⟫•◦•⟪———————

Walter Deuel realized that the only way to keep his client from the chair was an insanity defense, so the Waite case triggered a nationwide debate about insanity and criminal responsibility.

Deuel hired Dr. Morris J. Karpas, who would, in the days leading up to the trial, probe the deepest recesses of Waite's psyche. Meanwhile, Swann employed three alienists, or mental health professionals, to determine Waite's ability to stand trial: Dr. William Mabon, Dr. Menas S. Gregory and Smith Ely Jelliffe. Dr. Gregory, the director of Bellevue's "psychopathic ward," had come to know Waite well over the previous week.

During the first week of April, the four men spent hours interviewing Waite. Reporters dogged them at every turn, doing their best to pry information from the alienists, but the experts remained tight-lipped.

One *New York Times* correspondent managed to corner Dr. Gregory on the steps of Bellevue, but his responses only deepened the mysteries about Waite's psyche. Dr. Gregory characterized Waite as "a very sick man," but when pressed about the details, he changed the subject. "It's a beautiful day," he mused.

Undaunted, the *Times* reporter asked, "But did you find any signs of insanity in him?"

The alienist smiled, looked around and cryptically responded, "Everywhere I look I see signs of insanity."[124]

⸻ ❖ ⸻

Waite sat up in bed and waited for the reporters to arrive. He had kept his distance from the press, but on Thursday, April 6, he agreed to grant a brief interview. Still weak from his overdose, Waite remained in bed when the parade of journalists flooded into his room in the alcoholics' ward of Bellevue Hospital.

The reporters, curious about the man who single-handedly pushed headlines about the Great War to the margins, formed a hollow circle around Waite's bed.

He appeared lucid, sullen and contrite. "I don't want to say anything that will in any way lessen the penalty I must pay or would in any way enable me to escape the fullest punishment. Society expects me to pay the price."

Waite gazed out the window.

"Are you insane?" one of the reporters asked.

"I suppose I am sane," he said, still staring out the window. "Of course I am sane. I am as sane as anybody on this earth."

Another reporter asked him about "the man from Egypt."

"I don't want to say anything about that," Waite answered flatly.

They asked him about his experimentation with germ cultures and his confession, but Waite would give nothing away. He answered with vague, evasive responses.

Eventually, a reporter asked about Margaret. "Did Mrs. Horton figure in your plans for the future?"

Waite refused to answer the question. He stared at the reporters for a few seconds. "I was absolutely alone in what I did," he said.

"You have confessed to poisoning two people and to planning to do away with a third. Did you plan to include Miss Catherine Peck in your list?"

Waite laughed. "You fellows have a great imagination."

One of the journalists asked Waite if he was bigamist. "I never have been married to but one woman."

"Then who is the woman who signs herself 'Your African Mother?'"

"I have some property in British East Africa. It is managed by a man named Steyn. His sixty-six-year-old mother is very fond of me, and I am very fond of her. She often signs her letters that way."

A few questions later, the twenty-five-minute interview ended. Waite shook the hand of each reporter as one by one they shuffled past his cot.

Even in his weakened state, Waite was impressive. "In each of his answers," wrote a *New York Tribune* reporter, "there shone the brilliancy of his egotism. His manner was that of a man who has accomplished something infinitely greater than the men who questioned him. He had experienced the great adventure; they had not."[125]

———⟡———

By the second week of April, Clara was still under the weather. Throughout the winter, she had felt drained of energy, which she attributed to nothing more than a mild cold that just refused to go away. Her malaise, however, had gone from bad to worse, undoubtedly caused by the stress of her ordeal.

But with all the headlines about Arthur's attempt to infect her parents and the news stories about Arthur's alleged admission of plotting to murder her, Clara began to wonder if Waite might have given her something, too. If he wanted to inherit her fortune, then, logically, she would have been next. Yet Arthur wasn't the most attentive husband. She didn't remember him ever serving her a cup of tea.

Nonetheless, she decided to err on the side of caution and asked Dr. Schurtz to make a house call and run some blood tests.

———⟡———

On April 18, Clara received a peculiar letter from Waite. The letter read like an obituary.

"The Bad, Little Black Man from Egypt is dead," Waite declared. "He died last Tuesday, and I honestly died with him. I suppose you would have been glad if I had."

After declaring his undying love, Waite complained about his headaches. "My brain aches so up in front," he said. "Things get dark."

"Do not try to forgive me—it would be impossible. My brain is purged at last. I am ready to meet my Maker if that should come, and if not, I shall do by silent thought and in whatever way I can conceive to make a little amends to the poor crushed soul of what was my Clara."[126]

Clara folded the note, shoved it into an envelope and addressed it to Mancuso. Then, she picked up the telephone and dialed Mancuso's number.

Mancuso chuckled after listening to Clara read the note aloud. To the assistant district attorney, the letter was another lame stratagem by a man desperate to prove insanity where none existed. Waite, it appeared, was still trying to use Clara.[127]

He stopped laughing when Clara explained that she had remembered a pertinent detail she wanted to share with the prosecutor—a detail she felt proved Waite tried to infect her, her father and her mother with dangerous bacteria. Waite kept two atomizers in their New York apartment: one that he kept in the refrigerator and another that he kept on a windowsill outside their bedroom.

When the Pecks came to town, Clara said, he took the elderly couple on long drives in his car. Once under full speed, he put down the windshield. The bitter, cold draft left them shivering.[128]

Then, when they returned to the Coliseum, Waite suggested they should do something to keep from catching colds. He said he had some sprays that would prevent such an illness. As a well-known, highly educated dental surgeon, they reasoned, Waite had access to the latest in medical technology. Without question, they followed his direction. Using the atomizers, he sprayed their nostrils and throats every night.

Clara told Mancuso that Waite also gave a tablet a day to her mother, and in the two days before Hannah Peck's death, he gave her a tablet every hour.

Mancuso relayed the conversation to Swann. Although the DA suspected Arthur had murdered Hannah Peck, he couldn't move on the case without concrete evidence to contradict her official cause of death. Besides, she had been cremated, so any physical evidence of murder would have gone up in smoke.

To his horror, Dr. Schurtz discovered the presence of both typhus and anthrax in Clara's blood. He arranged for Clara to go to a sanatorium in Fraser, Indiana, and then addressed the media. He explained why Waite's plan to poison Clara had failed.

"Mrs. Waite's physical condition was very good, and that fact alone kept the number of Waite's murders down. Also, the conditions at the Coliseum apartment were not ideal for the keeping of cultures, and many of the germs in the atomizers were dead when injected. If the cultures had been virulent, there is no question in my mind that Clara would have died about the same time that her father did, and arsenic would never have been necessary in taking Peck's life."[129]

Meanwhile, the revelations continued to flood into Swann's office. Mancuso uncovered evidence that Waite had fooled around with five other women while courting Clara. Each of the women came from the economic elite, prompting Mancuso to label Waite a "love pirate." When not busy bedding debutantes in New York, Mancuso discovered, Waite cavorted with at least six more women in other cities. Waite, however, appeared more interested in their bank accounts than their beds. He primarily played with economically well-fixed women.[130]

The negative publicity didn't hurt Margaret Horton's career. She turned her attention to vaudeville and was offered a spot in a show at Loew's American Music Hall. On Friday, May 5, crowds overwhelmed the theater to watch her debut performance.

A throng rushed under the music hall marquee, which advertised "the beautiful and accomplished Mrs. Margaret Horton of the Waite case."

Mrs. Horton sang a few songs and left the stage but returned following a rousing ovation. She did not, however, impress the *New York Dramatic Mirror* theater critic, who panned the headliner's performance. He characterized it as "without expression, in a strong but uncertain voice."

He also hated the obvious fact that she, and the theater, banked on her notoriety. "We have no patience with commentators who declare that Mrs. Horton was booked on merit," the critic wrote. "We take decided exception to the way she was advertised and billed. Moreover, the booking of anyone upon unsavory newspaper notoriety does a positive injury to vaudeville. Indeed, the varieties took a step backward with Mrs. Horton's appearance."[131]

—————⇒•⇐—————

By mid-May, Clara had recovered fully and made the trip to New York, where she waited for the beginning of what she knew would become a trial circus. For two months, the case had been yesterday's news; now, it would once again become front-page fodder. And once again, she would become a major figure in the public eye and be forced to rehash her fairy tale romance for all to hear. It had become a twisted fairy tale, like some cautionary story conjured by the Brothers Grimm to warn young, gullible trust-fund princesses about their Prince Charming suitors.

A combination of factors—illness, embarrassment and reticence born of alleged misquotes by sensationalized accounts—had caused Clara to shy away from reporters, but on the eve of the trial, Clara sat for an interview. Nervous, she rubbed her hands together as she spoke.

In her statement, Clara chastised Margaret Horton and indicted all Big Apple women for their loose morality: "I am different from the women of New York. I blame the women here as well as the husbands they entangle. Mrs. Horton knew my husband was married. If New York is to be better, its women must reform. Personally, I care nothing about the Horton woman. I never think of her."

The reporter looked up from his notebook and stared straight into Clara's eyes.

"I think she ought to be punished, yes, but I will take no action against her."

Clara looked out the window and paused. She would have accepted "another woman" as the inevitable consequence of wedding a hunk. "Dr. Waite could have had her and a thousand like her if only he had spared me my parents. He has taken those I loved most and he might as well have taken me. I believe he would have done so eventually if he had not been discovered. Life holds nothing for me now."

"But Mrs. Waite…"

Clara interrupted the reporter, holding up her index finger as if scolding a recalcitrant child. "Dr. Waite is no longer my husband. He ceased to be a long time ago." Clara explained that even though her divorce was not yet final, she considered it a done deal.

She also said that she knew Arthur was "perfectly sane" and said she would willingly testify against him. "There is something that is urging me," she said. "I cannot express exactly what I mean—it is as if my dead parents were directing me to appear as their representatives against the man who coldly and cruelly killed them."[132]

"The man from Egypt" had returned.

PART II

TRIAL AND AFTERMATH

THE CASE AGAINST WAITE

NEW YORK, NEW YORK,

Monday, May 22–Tuesday, May 23, 1916[133]

The sun was shining in Manhattan when Arthur Warren Waite crossed the Bridge of Sighs on his way to the Criminal Branch of the Supreme Court. Grinning ear to ear, Waite felt confident he would beat the rap. After what he had to say on the stand, he was certain the jurors would find him insane despite what the newsmen had written.

It was a crime "worthy of the Borgias," wrote the *New York Herald* correspondent at the outset of the trial, "though prompted solely by an unbridled lust for money."[134] The *Herald* writer joined a cadre of journalists from Grand Rapids as well as New York who waited for Waite to make his entrance.

Clara Peck, who had dropped the "Waite" and reverted to her maiden name, sat alongside her brother, Percy, and his wife. In another section of the courtroom, Warren Waite sat with his son Frank.

Several doctors and alienists also sat in the gallery. As the trial progressed, they would study the defendant, noting anything—from facial expressions to physical movements—that provided hints about his psychosis. Doctors working for the prosecution would look for signs of sanity, while doctors working for the defense wanted to prove them wrong.

Just before 10:00 a.m., Swann entered the courtroom alongside Assistant District Attorney George N. Brothers and co-counsels Francis X. Mancuso and John T. Dooling. Brothers, a tenacious litigator, would handle questioning for the prosecution. Walter Rogers Deuel, with young attorney Joseph Force Crater as his second chair, appeared for the defense.

Waite photographed during a break in the court action. *From the Bain News Service, Library of Congress.*

All five attorneys sharply stood to attention with almost military precision as Justice Clarence J. Shearn walked into the courtroom. Shearn nodded to the court clerk, William Penney.

"Arthur W. Waite to the bar," Penney bellowed.

Waite strode into the courtroom with the same long gait he used when stepping onto the tennis court. Tall and lanky, he stood half

Frank Waite (left) and Warren Waite (right) photographed during Arthur's trial. *From the Bain News Service, Library of Congress.*

a head taller than the officer who escorted him from his cell in the Manhattan City Prison, better known by its ominous nickname, the Tombs. He smiled—the signature smile that had opened many doors and even more blouses.

Clara watched him take his seat and remembered how that smile once made her weak in the knees. Now, the expression just turned her stomach.

Jury selection began promptly at ten o'clock. Crater and Waite whispered to each other while Deuel and Brothers questioned potential jurors about their views on capital punishment and mental instability.

Eventually, the lawyers agreed on the first juror, a fifty-five-year-old mechanical engineer named Robert Neill. Following tradition, Waite stood, faced Neill and listened as the court clerk uttered, "Juror, look upon the defendant. Defendant, look upon the juror." Awkwardly, the two men eyed each other for a few seconds before Neill took the first seat in the jury box and jury selection continued.

The press made much about Waite's reaction to the response of one prospective juror, an insurance agent named Robert Irving.

"Mr. Irving, are you opposed to capital punishment?" Mr. Brothers asked.

"Not in a case like this. I am very much in favor of it."[135]

Acutely aware of the alienists in the audience, Waite laughed aloud, so loud, in fact, that everyone in the courtroom—including Justice Shearn—turned and stared at him. From the outset, it appeared, Waite was going to try for some type of insanity defense.

When Irving expressed his disgust with how the courts treated criminals such as Waite and said he would not be inclined "to show this prisoner any leniency whatever," the court thanked him for his time, dismissed him and called the next candidate.

By one o'clock, the lawyers had managed to empanel a jury. Although Brothers and Deuel questioned fifty-six potential jurors, jury selection took just three hours—the fastest of any trial in the long history of criminal law in New York City.[136]

Robert Neill would preside as foreman over a group that included a merchant, a building superintendent, a secretary, an entrepreneur, an insurance agent, two brokers, an accountant, a manager, an electrical engineer, a real estate agent and a writer.[137] Only two of the jurors were unmarried, which Deuel feared might harm his playboy client's case, and only three of the jurors were under forty.

After jury selection, Shearn adjourned for lunch.

———◆———

The afternoon session opened with Swann's thirty-five-minute summary of the prosecution's evidence.

Warren and Frank Waite watched the proceedings from the front row in the gallery.[138] Nervous, Warren fidgeted—a gesture carefully described by the *New York Herald* correspondent. "The father's gnarled hands, hands that worked hard that the son might be educated, clinched and the fingers laced and interlaced themselves, his wrinkled features working in suppressed emotion as District Attorney Swann in plain colors painted the horrid picture of the son's heartless and sordid crime."[139]

Percy, who wore a black arm band, and Ella, in a black taffeta dress, glared at Waite from their spot in the gallery as Swann approached the jury to give his opening statement.

The district attorney waltzed over to the jury box, took a deep breath and began.

"Gentlemen of the jury, we have the trial of an indictment for murder in the first degree against the defendant, Arthur Warren Waite. That indictment charges him with the murder of his father-in-law, John E. Peck, on the twelfth day of March, 1916. The criminal agency alleged in that indictment is the use of arsenic."

Waite listened, his head drooping slightly, as Swann addressed the jury. Although still smiling, Waite's pale complexion betrayed his appearance of suave indifference.

Swann outlined the state's case. After giving a brief biography of the man in the dock, he detailed Waite's scheme to murder his father-in-law to gain control over his wife's inheritance—a plot that included "live cultures" of "typhoid and pneumonia, diphtheria and other deadly diseases" that he mixed into John Peck's food and ninety grains of arsenic that he stirred into cups of tea and eggnog. The coup de grace, Swann noted, was a chloroform-soaked handkerchief and a pillow.

The district attorney had clearly made an impression on the defendant. The *Evening Telegram* reporter described Waite during the DA's opening: "As Mr. Swann's address continued Waite's appearance underwent a decided change. From the cheerful, carefree and erect young man of the forenoon session, he drooped visibly. His head sank forward so that his gaze rested on the table before him. The color faded from his face, leaving it deathly pale. The relatives of the dentist were affected visibly. Warren Waite, of Grand Rapids, father of the defendant, was seen to brush away tears."[140]

As for motive, Swann said, it was all done "for the purpose of obtaining money." He placed both hands on the rail, leaned forward and scanned the faces of the jurors. "Now gentlemen, that is the case of the People."[141] He bowed his head slightly and returned to his seat.

Court clerk William Penney announced the first witness in a booming voice that filled the courtroom: "Dr. Albertus Adair Moore." Throughout

Swann's opening address, Clara Peck's nerves frayed. As Moore walked to the witness stand, she retreated from the courtroom, disappearing through a side door.

As the physician who attended John Peck, Dr. Moore described the various visits he made to the Coliseum apartment and John Peck's seemingly minor illness.

During the first visit on March 5, Peck appeared fine except for a mild case of indigestion, which Peck attributed to eating oysters or "something that disagreed with him." Two days later, on March 7, he returned because Clara had become alarmed when Peck fainted in the bathroom. Dr. Moore, however, noticed nothing unusual except a slightly elevated heartbeat.

Dr. Moore dropped in on Peck over the next two days, but his patient still suffered from a bad case of diarrhea, so Moore put him on a diet and told the Waites that they could give him an occasional shot of brandy or whiskey.[142] Peck's pulse was a little rapid, but his temperature was normal.

Two days later, at about noon on Saturday, March 11, Dr. Moore saw John Peck alive for the last time. Except for the same slightly rapid pulse, he appeared in good condition. He complained about cabin fever and wanted to get outside. Moore assured him that if he felt better the next day, he could go out for a walk or a ride.

Waite, Moore said, was very anxious about John Peck's condition. Waite, Moore recalled, "asked me if I thought he [Peck] was in any serious condition, and I said, 'No, I think he will soon be out again.'"

Late that night, five minutes before one o'clock on Sunday morning, a ringing telephone jarred Dr. Moore from a deep slumber. It was Waite. "I have been trying to get you for some little time," Waite said. "Mr. Peck—I am afraid something has happened to Mr. Peck. It seems to me that he has died."

Moore was stunned by the news. "My Lord, doctor, surely nothing serious has happened," he remarked. He couldn't believe it and suggested Waite return and check Peck's pulse again while he waited on the line. "I held the wire," Moore explained, "and he came back and said that he was afraid that the worst had happened."

Moore got dressed and went to the Coliseum, arriving at about 1:45 a.m.

Waite met him at the door. "There is no change in his condition?" Moore asked. "No, I think he has gone," Waite responded.

At this point in Moore's testimony, Waite had grown tired and began to doze, but Joseph Force Crater prodded him. The incident didn't escape notice by a *New York Herald* reporter. "Mr. Crater," he wrote in his notebook, "touched his [Waite's] elbow and he started like a sleepy man does in church when he is caught napping."[143]

Brothers then asked Moore to recall statements he heard Waite make to Detective Cunniff about purchasing arsenic at John Peck's request. Deuel shot from his seat and screamed, "Objection!" After a heated exchange, Shearn allowed the question to stand.

"He said, in answer to a question," Dr. Moore recalled, "that he had not given Mr. Peck the arsenic; that the old man, as he expressed it, the old man must have taken it himself because he did not want to live."[144]

As Moore stepped down from the witness box, Justice Shearn glanced at his pocket watch. It was five o'clock, so he decided to adjourn for the day. Before dismissing the jury, Shearn warned them: "During this trial, I will not ask you gentlemen to refrain from reading the newspaper. I am not going to put you in the custody of the sheriff. I will put you on your honor, so that you may go about your business. If anyone speaks to you about this trial you are to report the fact to me."[145]

Moore's testimony provided the perfect opening act for the prosecution, and everyone was curious about how Waite's defense would attempt to use alleged insanity to sidestep a death sentence.

As the parties withdrew from the courtroom, a reporter overheard one of Swann's assistants speculate about Waite's likely insanity defense: "There is no such thing as impulsive insanity. As the name implies, its victims commit crimes on impulses beyond their control. 'Compulsive insanity,' I believe, will be held up as opposed to impulsive—the victim being driven to crime by stress of circumstance."[146]

———❧———

That evening, while Waite whiled away the hours in his Tombs cell, Clara agreed to an interview with a *New York Tribune* reporter. She asked as many questions as the reporter. She wanted to know how Arthur's father was doing, but she didn't ask a single question about Arthur, which struck the reporter as odd.

"I do not feel even curious about him," Clara explained. "It isn't that the man I loved is gone, it's that he never lived. That is what is hardest of all."

Clara said that even when the evidence began to pile up, she stayed by her man. Eventually, though, she had to admit his guilt. "I had just a little more than three months of married life, and I was happy every moment." She smiled. "Arthur was a wonderful lover. Think of awaking from a dream like that to such a terrible reality."

Clara was particularly interested in Margaret Horton. She had more in common with "Mrs. Walters" than she cared to admit. Both had been charmed into an embarrassing situation by Arthur Warren Waite's irresistible smile. Both shared a childlike naïveté that made them putty in the hands of a gifted con man like Waite. Clara spent most of her youth in the sheltered world of the wealthy, prompting Dr. Perry Schurtz to characterize her as a fourteen-year-old when it came to worldly sophistication. Margaret, according to Harry Mack Horton, was a dove among the predatory crows of New York.

"Tell me what she looks like," Clara pleaded. She listened intently as the reporter described the attractive singer.

"I knew she must be pretty. I couldn't have believed that there could have been another woman in Arthur's life," she remarked. "He said his one thought was to please me, and to be a better husband."

Arthur, Clara went on, was a good husband, and despite what appeared in the papers about their courtship, Arthur was her choice as well as her mother's. She really did love him, she explained, and then, like a little girl showing off her prize, she asked the reporter one last question: "Isn't he good looking?"[147]

<hr />

After a good night's rest in the Tombs, Waite returned to the courtroom on Tuesday morning, May 23, 1916, with a bounce in his step. He pranced into the courtroom with the sang-froid of a man who just stepped onto the tennis court for a friendly match.

"Dr. Waite," an *Evening Telegram* reporter commented, "entered the court room jauntily, briskly, marching a few steps ahead of the two deputy sheriffs who had him in custody. He seated himself vigorously at the counsel table, shaking hands with his counsel, Walter R. Deuel and Joseph Crater, and nodding cheerily to Warren Waite, his father, and Frank Waite, his brother."[148]

The gallery was filled to capacity with friends, family, reporters and a few curious observers who managed to find seats, which wasn't easy. "The cordon of police officers at the door," noted the *Evening Telegram* correspondent, "kept away most of those who applied for admission." Among the new faces in the crowd were several witnesses for the prosecution and a few friends and family members who didn't sit in on the first day of the trial. Catherine Peck sat next to her nephew Percy and his wife. "All were dressed in deep mourning," the *Evening Telegram* correspondent commented.

Majestic edifice of the City Prison, better known by its ominous nickname, the Tombs.
From the Detroit Publishing Company, Library of Congress.

Swann devoted the morning session to medical testimony designed to show that Waite first poisoned John Peck with a fatal amount of arsenic and then, becoming impatient, finished the job by smothering him.

Dr. Victor C. Vaughn, the dean of the University of Michigan's Medical School in Ann Arbor, took the stand. As the doctor sat down, an assistant placed two jars containing organs removed from John Peck's body. This delighted the members of the press, who jotted descriptions of the morbid evidence in their notebooks while Vaughn testified about his discovery of arsenic in John Peck's remains.

Vaughn then held up a vial of pink-colored fluid he received from Dr. Otto H. Schultze. This, he explained, was the fluid Kane used in embalming John Peck, and it contained no arsenic. This piece of evidence destroyed any possible defense that the presence of poison was a result of the embalmer's work.[149]

Dr. Otto H. Schultze, "medical assistant to the district attorney of New York County," testified after Vaughn. He described the second autopsy done on John Peck's remains in the "autopsy room" of Sprattler's mortuary in Grand Rapids. He removed the brain, the remainder of the intestines and the throat structures. He placed them in jars and sent them to Dr. Stanley Benedict, a chemistry professor at Cornell University.

"Doctor," George Brothers asked, "from the examination that you made of John E. Peck at Grand Rapids during the autopsy which you performed there, did you find any evidence then of his death from natural causes?"

Schultze grinned and shook his head slowly. "I did not."

Brothers asked what, in Schultze's opinion, caused John Peck's death.

"Poisoning by white arsenic, arsenic trioxide."[150]

Swann devoted the next phase of his case to a sequence of witnesses who would prove Waite purchased the arsenic used to murder John Peck.

Dr. Richard W. Muller testified that on March 9, Waite asked for help in acquiring a package of arsenic. "He said he had been sleepless for several nights on account of the yelling of the cats in his yard," Dr. Muller said, "and he wanted to kill them, and I sympathized with him because I had been in a same condition."[151] Muller phoned Richard H. Timmerman, a pharmacist who agreed to sell Waite the poison.

Timmerman followed Dr. Muller to the stand and described Waite's March 9 visit to his pharmacy. He asked Waite why he wanted arsenic, and Waite repeated the tale about noisome cats. "So," Timmerman said, "I suggested to the defendant: 'Why not use strychnine?'"

"What did the defendant say to your suggestion?"

"He said, no, he would rather have arsenic." There were a few gasps from the gallery. Although a more effective cat killer, strychnine would have caused symptoms that would have been harder for Waite to conceal.

Timmerman asked his clerk, Robert Schmadel, to make the sale, which he documented in the "poison register."

Brothers entered Timmerman's "poison register" into evidence and asked the pharmacist to identify the line recording the sale, including the name

Famed New York medical examiner Dr. Otto Schultze. Although Waite confessed to smothering John E. Peck, Dr. Schultze believed that Peck died as the result of arsenic poisoning. *From the Bain News Service, Library of Congress.*

"A.W. Waite," his address, "poison—arsenic" and the quantity—a dram and a half or ninety grains.

Brothers read from the book: "A dram and a half. Purpose for which it is to be used: poison sick cat. Name of dispenser: Robert Schmadel. Witness: R. Timmermann. Number of sale: 117."[152]

Richard C. Schmadel, an assistant pharmacist, took the stand after his boss. The clerk verified vital details of Timmerman's testimony, including his boss's suggestion that Waite purchase strychnine. He also verified that the "poison register" came from Timmerman's Lexington Avenue shop.

After Schmadel stepped down from the stand, the morning session ended, and Waite returned to the Tombs for lunch.

⟫•◦•⟪

All eyes watched as Margaret Horton, flanked by her sister Helen and two friends—Dorothy Von Palmenberg and Aimee Crocker Gouraud Mishkinoff, known throughout New York high society as "Princess Mishkinoff"— waltzed into the courtroom just before Waite returned from the Tombs.

The *Evening Telegram* reporter described the curious figure: "She was pale, but did not appear worried. She smiled at some acquaintances as she entered the courtroom and quietly took a seat near the rear of the room. The gaze of spectators appeared to annoy her, as she inclined her head so that the big drooping brim of her black straw hat hid her face."

As soon as Waite entered the courtroom, he recognized his "studio companion," but she gave him the cold shoulder—a gesture not missed by the *Evening Telegram* journalist. "Mrs. Horton, standing in the court room this afternoon, turned her back deliberately when Waite approached on his way from the Tombs, where he had luncheon. The prisoner passed within five feet of the woman for whom he hired an apartment in the Plaza, but gave no sign of recognizing her."[153]

After Dr. Jacob B. Cornell briefly testified about the icy reception he received from Waite when he came to pay his respects, Swann called the one witness who had seen Waite and Margaret Horton together.

As Arthur Swinton rose from the gallery and headed toward the witness stand, Margaret Horton slipped out of the courtroom. A nephew of Dr. Jacob B. Cornell, Swinton was lunching at the Plaza with his sister and mother when they bumped into Waite.

"Was he alone or accompanied?" Brothers asked.

"No, he was with a lady," Swinton said.

"Do you know the lady?"

"I think I could identify her, but I hadn't seen her before that time."

Brothers turned to face the gallery. "Is Mrs. Margaret Horton here?"

The room fell silent. People in the gallery searched for Waite's Juliet, but she was nowhere to be seen. Brothers turned back to Swinton. "Could you describe the appearance of the lady?"

Swinton described her as wearing a white suit and a large white hat and carrying "white fox furs." Waite, Swinton testified, "told us that he had just performed a delicate operation in Bellevue Hospital, and that he had his private nurse with him, that he had come uptown in his machine and had stopped at the Plaza for a bite to eat before he performed another operation at the Astor Private Hospital."[154]

As Swinton left the stand, Margaret Horton tiptoed back into the courtroom.

The day's most eagerly anticipated witness took the stand in the last hour of the afternoon session.

"Eugene O. Kane," Penney bellowed. The embalmer stood and quickly shuffled across the floor to the witness box.

This sketch by *New York Herald* artist J.C. Fireman shows notables in the gallery watching the trial drama unfold. *From the Wednesday, May 24 edition of the* New York Herald.

To avoid incriminating Kane as an accomplice after the fact and to avoid marring his witness's already-questionable credibility, Brothers carefully framed his questions. He asked Kane to detail his methods and the contents of his embalming fluid. Kane listed the ingredients.

"Any arsenic in it?" Brothers asked.

"No, sir."

"Was there any arsenic in the embalming fluid that you injected into the body of John E. Peck on March 12 of this year?"

"Absolutely not."

Kane described the attempted bribe. After he detailed the ingredients of his embalming fluid to Waite, Waite asked, "'Could there be arsenic put into it?' I told him it could be, but it was against the law, and I would not do such a thing as that, and that was about all that was said in regard to that at that time."

Kane did not state that Waite paid him to say he used arsenic in the embalming process—which would implicate him—but Brothers scored points with the jury when Kane described the pay-off. Waite, Kane explained, handed him a check and said, "That is for you" and then told him "he could put me on easy street for life." He tried to give the check back, but Arthur Warren Waite wasn't one to take "no" for an answer. Kane pocketed the check, but, he said, he later destroyed it.

Brothers then asked Kane to describe the meeting at the cigar store on Fifty-Ninth Street. Kane said he went into the phone booth and stood next to Waite. "I had on a large gray ulster unbuttoned and he came up in front of me and pushed this small bundle in my inside coat pocket."

"What did he push into your pocket?"

"It was money, a roll of money."

Kane struggled through his answers, pausing, choosing his words carefully to avoid any hint of wrongdoing. Waite enjoyed watching the undertaker sweat.

The *New York Tribune* writer studied Waite's reaction to Kane's testimony. Waite grinned with "the pleased smile with which a Roman Emperor of similar humorous sense might have viewed a race between a sacrificial slave and a hungry lion."[155]

"What did he say as he pressed this bundle into your pocket?"

"'For God's sake, get some of that arsenic into that fluid and send it down to the district attorney's office—as soon as possible.' I think he said that."[156]

On cross-examination, Deuel asked the embalmer just two questions.

"Did you ever find the other $1,200?" he asked, referring to the amount missing from the $9,000 bankroll Waite stuffed into his jacket pocket.

"I don't know," Kane shrugged and managed a slight smile.

Deuel fired the second question at the embarrassed embalmer: "Were you ever convicted of a crime?"

"Yes," Kane blushed. The undertaker had done time following a conviction for bigamy—a prior bad act reported throughout the city's newspapers.[157]

Deuel didn't probe. He had accomplished what he wanted: the jury heard the witness state that he had a record, which injured his credibility. "That is all," Deuel said.

Deuel faced an uphill battle, and he knew it. In just two days of testimony, prosecution witnesses had proven that John Peck had ingested a fatal dose of arsenic, that Waite had purchased arsenic just days before Peck's death and that Waite had attempted to manufacture evidence through Eugene Oliver Kane.

It had been a bad two days for the defense, but the most damaging testimony was yet to be heard.

12

WITNESS FOR THE PROSECUTION

NEW YORK, NEW YORK
Wednesday, May 24, 1916

At the onset of the trial's third day, the key characters in the drama took their seats in the gallery. Percy Peck sat next to Aunt Catherine and Elizabeth Hardwicke, who would step up onto the witness stand and solve one of the lingering mysteries in the case. Harry Mack Horton escorted his wife, Margaret, into the courtroom, where they sat in the back row, as far from the Peck family as space allowed.

Reporters eagerly awaited Swann's lineup of prosecution witnesses. The first two days provided little that hadn't made it into the papers in March, but on the third day, the women in Waite's life would testify against him. Clara would describe life with her charlatan husband; Margaret, reporters hoped, would titillate the audience with stories about her behind-closed-door doings with Waite; and the mysterious "K. Adams," who sent the telegram that caused Waite's perfect murder plot to collapse like a house of cards, would be unveiled.

Waite, perhaps more than anyone in the courtroom, realized just how damaging the upcoming testimony would be to his case. As Sheriff Whitman escorted him into the courtroom, he remarked, "Oh, what's the use of this farce? They could have finished the whole thing in an hour."[158]

Every reporter in the courtroom turned and stared at the figure who stood when Penney announced "Elizabeth Hardwicke."

The niece of Dr. Jacob Cornell, Elizabeth Hardwicke's turn on the stand lasted just two minutes—long enough to reveal herself as the author of the mysterious "K. Adams" telegram. When her uncle had returned from the

Percy S. Peck posed for this photograph during the trial of Arthur Warren Waite. *From the Bain News Service, Library of Congress.*

Waite apartment on March 12 and described Arthur's odd demeanor, she became suspicious. Her doubts escalated when her cousin Arthur Swinton described his chance meeting with Arthur and his gorgeous "nurse" at the Plaza. Based on intuition alone, she began to suspect foul play.

"Is this the telegram which you wrote and handed in to the clerk, Exhibit 41 for identification?" Brothers handed Hardwicke the telegram.

She read over the note carefully and handed it back to Brothers. "It is."

"Did anybody ask you to send that?"

"Yes."

Deuel objected, and the court sustained. Brothers ended his line of questions, and Elizabeth Hardwicke stepped down without revealing who spurred her to write the "K. Adams" telegram. Nevertheless, the question of the identity of "K. Adams" had finally been publicly laid to rest.[159] The irony that Waite's grand scheme collapsed due to a female's intuition did not escape notice by reporters in the courtroom, who would later characterize the young socialite as a true hero in the case.

All eyes were fixed on the mysterious "K. Adams," so no one noticed when a side door opened slightly and a slim figure squeezed inside. Clara Louise Peck took a seat behind the jury box, screened from view of the spectators.

A few seconds later, Penney summoned her to the witness stand: "Clara Louise Peck."

People in the back of the gallery stood and craned their necks to catch a glimpse of Clara as she made her way to the stand. Waite, however, dropped his head and slapped his palm over his eyebrows in an attempt to shield his face. He looked like a man saluting his shoes.

The *New York Evening Telegram* correspondent described Clara: "She was attired in deep mourning with a veil draped over a large hat." The brim of the hat was so broad, noted the *Sun* correspondent, that it obscured Clara's view of the entire right side of the room, including her husband.

Clara took her seat, folded her hands in her lap and turned her gaze toward Brothers.

Through his line of questions, Brothers planned to create a narrative of John Peck's last few days inside the Waite apartment.

Clara spoke in a barely audible tone. In fact, she spoke so softly that the jurors were having trouble hearing her. Juror Number Twelve, a writer named Joseph Trant, asked that she speak up.

"Do you think if you raise your veil you could speak a little louder?" Brothers asked, but Clara shook her head. She would not unveil herself to the courtroom. "No, I think I can do all right."

Brothers continued. "What was your father's health when he arrived at your home on that visit?"

Clara cleared her throat and did her best to speak loud enough for the jury to hear. "He had a slight cold, but that was all." About ten days before

Clara Peck Waite (right) poses alongside Elizabeth Hardwicke (left), aka "K. Adams." *From the Bain News Service, Library of Congress.*

he died, Clara explained, John Peck's cold turned into a serious stomachache that climaxed when, on March 7, he collapsed on the bedroom floor.

Then, suddenly, on March 8, his condition improved. As the day progressed, he appeared to grow stronger.

The next day, Dora Hillier's day off, Clara prepared a meal of pea soup, oysters, beefsteak and potatoes. Waite helped by carrying the soup and oysters to the table.

Brothers paused, and the spectators fell silent. This, they realized, was when Waite spiked John Peck's soup with arsenic.

After dinner, John Peck felt sleepy and went to bed. The next morning, he woke up feeling fine, so that afternoon, Clara went out to do a little shopping. When she returned about five o'clock, she discovered that "he had a bad spell" and had begun vomiting. As the evening progressed, his "vomiting spells" increased.

On Saturday morning, March 11, Clara went to her father's room as soon as she awoke "to see if he had had a good night." She described his condition. "He looked very weak, and he had had several spells in the night. He said he had a very bad night." Nonetheless, Peck managed to climb out of bed and dress, but he spent most of the day on a divan in the front room. Both Clara and Arthur stayed home all day to watch over him.

At one point—at about three o'clock in the afternoon—John Peck became so weak, he returned to his bedroom to lie down. After napping a few hours, he returned to the sofa in the front room.

Brothers asked Clara what her father had to eat that day. "Saturday noon I made my father an eggnog." Peck took a few sips but couldn't down the entire mug, so Clara put it in the icebox. That was the only eggnog she had prepared, Clara testified, and she gave him the eggnog just that one time, at noon.

Peck was too sick to eat dinner, and at about five o'clock, he returned to his bedroom. As Clara helped him along, Peck complained about bitter stomach pains. "My father told me that he had had the eggnog and not to give him any more, it had made him sick."

Tears rolled down Clara's cheeks. She wiped her face with the back of her hand.

Deuel vigorously contested John Peck's statement about the eggnog, and after several objections, Shearn struck it out. Despite the judge's ruling, however, the jury heard about the remark. Clara said she didn't give her father the eggnog that evening, and John Peck was too weak to help himself. There was only one logical conclusion: Waite gave Peck the eggnog, which probably contained a large amount of white arsenic.

Brothers resumed his questions. "What time did you go to bed?"

"About ten o'clock."

"Before going to bed, did you say good night to your father?"

Clara choked back a tear. Brothers handed her a handkerchief, which she used to wipe her nose. "I did."

It seemed like a good time for a break, so Justice Shearn decided to adjourn for the noon recess.[160]

———◆———

News leaked from the courthouse that Margaret Horton would take the stand after Clara, and a crowd of mostly women gathered outside the courtroom. The special detail of police tasked with keeping curious onlookers outside held back the throng and admitted only witnesses, family members and reporters.

Clara returned to the witness stand, this time with her veil removed. She kept her face partially hidden by her broad-brimmed hat.

Summoning all of her strength, Clara resumed her testimony by recalling the events the night her father died.

Waite, Clara testified, suggested that he spend the night on the sofa, which he had placed outside of John Peck's bedroom. "[H]e said I have been through so much that I needed a good night's rest, so he would be near my father, if he wanted anything."

"Do you recall waking up during the night?"

"Yes, sir. Dr. Waite came and woke me up about half past one."

"And when you were aroused, you found Dr. Waite by your side. Is that right?"

"Yes, sir."

"What did he say to you?"

Clara took a deep breath in an attempt to keep from crying. "He said that Mr. Peck had had a very bad night."

For the first time during her testimony, Clara's emotions spilled over. Her lips quivered and tears welled up at the corners of her eyes, spilling down her cheeks and forming lines across her face. She buried her head in her hands and sobbed.

After a few seconds, Clara regained her composure and was ready to continue.

"Did you ever accompany him to any hospital?" Brothers asked.

On several occasions, Clara said, she went along with Waite to hospitals, but she never actually went inside. She described one instance. When Hannah Peck came to visit in January, Waite took them to Cornell, "and he went inside and was gone about twenty minutes and came out and told us about a young fellow who had broken his jaw up here"—Clara pointed to a spot on her upper jaw—"and that it is so hard to heal, he said, the accident was so great."[161]

As she described the incident, Clara thought of how proud she was of Arthur. He worked so hard. Every morning, he left the house to go to work. He rarely came home for lunch and often left unexpectedly in the evening to tend to a patient. He even once asked Clara to give him a dress as a gift for a "charity patient."

After Waite's arrest, it became clear to Clara that Waite wasn't interested in philanthropy but in philander. Waite's fictitious business provided the ideal cover for his trysts. Clara looked at the back row of the courtroom, where Margaret Horton sat next to her husband. She wondered if Margaret Horton's trousseau once contained her charity dress.

Deuel began his cross-examination at about 3:15 p.m. by taking Clara down memory lane. He asked Clara to recall New Year's Eve 1914. "Did you have any conversation with him of a special nature?"

"Well, perhaps you would call it special."

That, Clara said, was the night Waite proposed. The edges of Clara's mouth curled up in a slight smile. The *New York Herald* correspondent captured Waite's demeanor at this moment: "There was an answering smile on the lips of Waite, but it was almost as sad a smile as hers."[162]

"Did you give him encouragement?" Deuel nudged.

Clara said she told Waite she greatly admired his accomplishments. Waite had "worked his way through college, for which I admired him very much," but she just couldn't commit to marriage at the time. Waite followed the Peck family south to Florida, where he pressed his suit. While there, Clara said, he won her affection.

Over the next few months, they continued a torrid courtship through the mail, writing two and sometimes three letters to each other a day. They had a lover's spat in July when Waite didn't write for three days. Clara traveled to New York, where she bumped into him at a house party. He gave her the cold shoulder, and she offered to return his engagement ring, but they ultimately decided to carry on with their relationship.

"What did he say about that engagement ring?"

"What did he say to me about it?"

Clara hesitated and looked away from Deuel. She blushed. "I do not know. Nothing—I do not recall particularly that he said anything, any more than any man would say when he presents an engagement ring to a girl."

After a little more prompting, Deuel managed to tease out a more specific answer.

"He said he would save money, and that he had hoped—that he had saved money so that when he did become engaged he could buy the girl that he cared for a very handsome ring."

Like the others in the courtroom, Margaret Horton watched the testimony with curiosity, but Clara's statement about the ring caused her to sit forward. The sense of déjà vu sent a chill down her spine. All of a sudden it occurred to her that she had, just a few months earlier, experienced a twisted version of Clara's engagement when Waite gave her a diamond ring. She wondered if the thought of New Year's Eve 1914 flashed across Waite's mind at the time.

Deuel shifted his line of questions to Waite's playacting as a physician. "What did he tell you he was doing for a living?"

"I understood when I married Dr. Waite that he was here in New York, practicing, working with other doctors."

As Waite listened to his wife's answer, a wry smile spread across his face.

"May I ask that the witness answer the question specifically, Your Honor?" Shearn looked at Clara. "Well, he told you that, did he?"

"He told me he was working here in New York as a physician."

Clara, at Deuel's prompting, described several incidents in which Waite claimed to have performed difficult surgeries throughout the city. Waite watched with amusement as Clara described the lengths he went to to deceive her.

On one occasion, "he told us that he had just performed, or he had just made a bridge work for a woman of sixty years of age, and this woman had had other bridge work done, but it had not been satisfactory and that the woman was very, very grateful to him for having given her such satisfaction," Clara said.

Waite slapped his hand over his mouth to avoid laughing aloud.

They lived the idyllic life, Clara said. Waite left home each morning to go to work but telephoned her every day and sometimes twice a day. He returned home for dinner every night, although he often stayed out on Thursdays.

Deuel asked Clara about Waite's attitude the night her father died. "Did he show emotion? Was he greatly affected by this demise and your suffering?"

"Yes. Dr. Waite said the night my father died, after Dr. Moore had left he came in my room and went to sleep and he was very sorry about my father's death, that he had thought so much of him himself. He was very sorry. That is all."[163]

With this last answer, Clara Louise Peck stepped down from the witness stand. It was 3:45 p.m. Her testimony consumed over three hours and spanned both the morning and afternoon sessions. She was exhausted. She slumped down in her chair next to the witness box.

"Margaret Horton," Penney bellowed. Everyone turned and looked to the back of the courtroom.

Waite's "studio companion" took the stand at about four o'clock. Everyone in the courtroom watched as she stood and strutted down the aisle. The *New York Herald* reporter described her as a "comely woman…effectively gowned in a tight-fitting crepe de Chine princess gown, set off at the breast with a white silk yoke, which was cut very low, revealing a shapely throat and neck, about which hung a rope of pearls."[164]

The *Evening Telegram* reporter described her as "a decided brunette… attired in a black silk gown relieved only by a rolling white collar, cut V shaped and very low at the throat. She wore a black straw hat with a wide brim."[165] The *Sun* writer described her gown as "low-cut."

On her way to the witness stand, Margaret Horton walked past Arthur Warren Waite, but despite his best efforts to make eye contact, she refused to look at him.

"Still waters run deep," Ray Schindler whispered as he watched the "dove among crows" make her way to the stand. Despite appearances, it was evident Margaret Horton did not want to testify against Waite. Her body language—from a wry smirk to the way she sashayed—sent a powerful message. Schindler had learned how to read this type of body language, which paid dividends when questioning female suspects and informants.

Brothers asked Margaret to describe how she first met the defendant. She explained that she first met him sometime between Christmas and New Year's Eve 1915. Clara smirked. This was when she was home in Grand Rapids, visiting her family.[166]

"After meeting the defendant at the Academy of Music, you and he became friendly?"

"Yes."

Brothers decided not to probe any further, to the dismay of reporters gathered in the gallery. The *Sun* reporter said, "Evidently Mr. Brothers was not going to be blunt in his questions," because he immediately took a different tack.

Brothers asked Margaret to describe her rendezvous with Waite on March 22—their tearful farewell at the Berlitz School.

Waite, Margaret recalled, asked her to go the drugstore for him and buy some medicine. Margaret said she watched as Waite wrote out the words "trional and sulphonal" on a piece of paper. He said he wanted a package of each drug. "He gave me a dollar and I went to the drugstore."

She returned to the Berlitz School and gave him the packages.

"What else did he say?"

Margaret glared at Brothers for a few seconds before answering. "He then ran up and down the steps a few minutes and I sat down, and he seemed excited, and I then asked him, I said, 'Doctor, I have seen now in the paper what they are accusing you of. You did not do that, surely, did you?' And he said 'Yes, I did.'"[167]

Several attendees gasped, followed by murmuring that grew to a crescendo of audible conversation. People familiar with the case knew that Margaret had changed her story. In March, she told reporters about the conversation but said that Waite had denied having a hand in the murders. Irritated with the noise coming from the gallery, Shearn tapped his gavel.

When the din quieted, Margaret went on to describe their farewell. "[Waite] gave me his ring, he threw his ring and some money in my lap." Waite's goodbye gift was a diamond ring. A few in the gallery turned and glanced at Harry Mack Horton, who squirmed and looked away.

"Do you remember his saying anything at that moment about the tablets?"

Margaret remembered that Waite mumbled "they are after me" and then "said something about doing away with himself before he allowed them to get him." She couldn't remember his actual words.

"Before he left you in the hall, did he say anything about seeing you again?"

Her voice dropped to a raspy whisper. "He said he perhaps would never see me again."

Brothers paused. His next line of questions was critical to smashing Waite's insanity defense.

"Did you receive, after he was arrested and while he was in Bellevue Hospital, any letter from him?"

Margaret leered at Brothers. "Yes, sir."

After a little cajoling from Brothers, Margaret explained that she had received two letters inked by Waite from Bellevue and delivered by Walter Deuel, who requested she burn them when finished. She showed the letters to her best friend, Mrs. Von Palmenberg, and then discarded them as directed.

"Will you try and remember, if you please, Mrs. Horton, what was in the letter, beginning at the beginning? What were the first words?"

"'Dear Margaret' were the first words." Her snide tone drew a few smiles from spectators.

"And then what was following that?"

"I can't recall just what followed."

Brothers wasn't going to take "no" for an answer. He couldn't. He needed the jury to hear what Waite said in that letter.

"Now, will you try," Brothers asked, "and remember as well as you can the substance of that letter?"

"He said something about having hurt the people that he loved the most."

"Do you remember whether anything was said about la chaise?"

"Oh yes."

"What was that?" Brothers asked.

"He said he did not suppose that he would get the la chaise or la sedia." Someone in the gallery whistled. Waite had apparently written to Margaret that the key to avoiding the electric chair—or "la sedia"—was convincing others he was insane.

"Did he say anything about an insane institution?"

"Yes."

"What was that?"

"He said he would probably go to an institution for a while and then get out."

There were a few murmurs from the gallery. Shearn hushed the onlookers with a tapping of his gavel.

"Did the jury hear?" Shearn asked. Several jurors bobbed their heads.

Brothers continued: "What did he say about the guards at Bellevue? You told us part of it. Can you remember the rest?"

"He said that he believed they thought he was insane."

"What else did he say about the guards, if anything?"

"I do not remember anything more." Margaret hoped Brothers would let it go, but somehow she knew he wouldn't.

"Did he say anything in the letter about your attitude?"

"Yes."

"What was that?"

"He said it was according to my attitude how he would act and feel."

"Did he explain what he meant by that in that letter?"

"He said that if I did not care for him anymore that I was to tell him so."

"And what else?"

"And that nothing would matter then."

"What?"

Margaret repeated her answer. "That nothing would matter then."

"Did he say anything in that letter that you recall about having them all guessing at Bellevue?"

"Yes, I think he said that."

"Did he say he was having lots of fun with the guards?"

"Yes."

"And he said, 'They all think I am crazy'?"

"Yes."

"Did he say anything about making a fight to live if you assured him that you still loved him?"

Margaret paused before answering. "Yes."

"Was the word 'Egypt' used in any of those letters?"

"Yes."

"And what was said about Egypt?"

"He said he supposed I had laughed at it."

"Laughed at what?" Brothers wanted the jury to hear it again.

"At 'the man from Egypt.'"

Shearn interrupted. The wording was vital, and he wanted a clarification for the jurors. "That you had laughed at it, or that you would laugh at it?"

"That I had laughed at it," Margaret answered, emphasizing the word "had."

"Was there anything said in any of the defendant's letters received by you from Mr. Deuel about four or forty years?"

"Yes," Margaret said, averting her eyes from the gallery.

"What was that?"

"I had said that to him."

"What did you say to him in your letter?"

"I do not recall just what I said, but I said something about waiting four or forty years."[168]

Again, several people in the gallery glanced to the back row, where Harry Horton sank lower in his seat.

With this last response, Brothers ended his direct examination, and Deuel stood to begin his cross. Deuel wanted to undo the impression that he had aided Waite in a scheme to engineer testimony by delivering Waite's letters. So he asked Margaret to describe the context of the letters. She explained that she had insisted on seeing Waite in Bellevue, but Deuel thought that it would bring negative publicity, so he suggested they communicate through notes that he agreed to deliver.

Deuel also wanted to quash any impression that he had helped to destroy evidence by telling her to burn the letters. Margaret explained that Deuel never ordered her to burn them; he said she could either destroy them or give them to him.

Under Deuel's questioning, Margaret rehashed her various interviews with John T. Dooling of the district attorney's office, including the six-hour marathon of March 25. Despite seemingly endless volleys of questions, Margaret said, the authorities still were not satisfied with her answers. They seemed hell-bent on a scenario in which Waite, after disposing of the Pecks, planned to whisk her away to a fairy tale life in an Italian castle. It didn't matter how many times she denied it; they just didn't seem to listen.

"Did you and Dr. Waite ever talk about going away together?"

"Never."

Then Deuel asked the one question on everyone's mind: "Were your relations with him purely platonic?"

Margaret nodded. "Yes." She went on to describe his behavior while at the Plaza as polite and mostly jovial, although he periodically suffered from fits of melancholy, particularly when she sang. In fact, she said, Waite cried every time she sang. For the most part, though, he was happy. He often said, "We are nothing but two children."[169]

Margaret's testimony—at an hour and twenty minutes—had consumed the remainder of the afternoon session. Her appearance—from her stunning, low-cut gown to her tone of voice—provided plenty of front-page fodder. "She used several accents before she finished her testimony," wrote the *Sun* reporter. "Starting with the broad 'a' she finally returned to the sharper twang of the middle West."[170] Margaret Horton, the *Sun* writer hinted, had used her time on the stand to showcase her talents.

The court adjourned for the day. Deuel managed to keep out of the record any references to Waite's procurement of dangerous disease germs, but Horton's testimony, particularly her recollection of Waite's love letters from Bellevue, was devastating. The next morning, Deuel would begin his case and do his best to keep Arthur Warren Waite off death row.

THE MORAL IMBECILE

NEW YORK, NEW YORK
Thursday, May 25–Friday, May 26, 1916

Walter Deuel had planned an insanity defense from the outset of the trial, but at the beginning of his case, he had to somehow undo the impression that Waite was merely feigning insanity to avoid a long prison sentence and "la chaise."

The only way to convince the jury that Waite wasn't faking was to put him on the stand, where he would give an elaborate confession of his misdeeds. The alienists in the audience would then surely label him insane, and the jury would send him to Matteawan, not Sing Sing. Waite's life now depended on his ability to act the part of a "moral imbecile."

Deuel first called Waite's father, Warren, and brothers, Frank and Clyde, to the stand. Warren Waite detailed Arthur's lifelong struggle with sticky fingers. He also hinted at the possibility that mental health issues ran in the family when he testified about Arthur's cousin Lillian Jackson, who died during a stint in an insane asylum, and another cousin who was presently institutionalized. Clyde Waite described an incident when his brother drowned a cat, but he couldn't remember any other acts of cruelty.

About midway through the afternoon session, at just after 3:00 p.m., Penney summoned the defendant: "Arthur Warren Waite."

The clerk's booming voice jarred Waite out of a nap. He stood, tugged on the tail of his coat jacket, smiled and walked to the witness stand. Several women in the crowd stood to see the infamous lady-killer.

Penney swore in the defendant. "Do you swear to tell the whole truth?"

Waite cocked his head slightly and grinned. "I do," he said in a teasing tone. He sat back in the chair, propped his arms on the armrests and crossed his legs. He didn't even glance at Clara, who sat just a few feet away. Clara dropped her head so the wide brim of her hat concealed her face.

The *Sun* correspondent described the scene: "The court room…was still as death. Jurors, wearied by the long session, sat bolt upright or leaned forward to catch every word."

Deuel began by quizzing Arthur about his long history of stealing things. As far back as he could remember, Arthur said, he stole. When he worked as a paperboy for the *Grand Rapids Herald*, he took extra copies that he would sell and pocket the proceeds. As a student at Grand Rapids High School, he sneaked up the fire escape and swiped a German examination from a teacher's desk. He never really studied in school, he said, instead spending his time playing baseball games.

The thefts, Waite explained, continued throughout college and his five years in South Africa, where he pilfered from his employer, Wellman & Bridgeman. Among other things, Waite said he stole "fine gold, which we used in casting, and so forth, some of which I brought back home here."

"Did you have any other kind of trouble while you were in South Africa?" Deuel asked.

Waite nervously repositioned himself in the chair. "One or two small matters."

"What were they?"

"Slightly unprofessional conduct with some of my patients."

"The nature of the unprofessional conduct?"

"Nothing more than flirtation."

"Did you have any trouble over a girl there?"

"Then, yes." Waite said some money exchanged hands to settle the affair "so that it would not be made public that I had done this."

Deuel turned to Waite's courtship of Clara.

Waite explained that he had returned to the United States in 1914. Upon a visit to Grand Rapids, Clara Louise Peck invited him to a reception. Enthralled with the Peck mansion, Waite became a frequent visitor after that.

"Were you in love with her?"

Waite shrugged. "I don't know."

In the gallery, Clara watched, a veil covering the tears that began to run down her cheeks.

"Can you state what the reason was for proposing marriage to her?"

"Money, possibly." Waite said he knew all about the Peck fortune, which was why he pursued Clara.

Grand Rapids High School, circa 1915, where Arthur Warren Waite went to school. On one occasion, Waite used the fire escape to enter a classroom and steal a German examination. *From the Detroit Publishing Company, Library of Congress.*

Deuel questioned Waite about his relationship with John Peck's sister, Catherine. Waite explained that he had completely duped Catherine into trusting him months before he married Clara. He lunched with her every noon—attention the elderly woman craved. Grateful, she lavished Waite with offers of money and expensive gifts, including jewelry. The gullible woman even gave him control over thousands of dollars in securities. Waite, however, insisted he didn't steal the money. "If I had spent the money," he said, "it would be theft. I misrepresented to her, but the money is still there—was still there."

He did, however, steal other things from Catherine Peck. On one occasion, he said, he plucked two $1,000 bonds from her trunk but returned them when she became suspicious. On another occasion, when Catherine left her rings unattended, he pried loose one of the diamonds and pocketed it.

As six thirty approached, Waite had spent two and a half hours on the stand. Exhausted, Deuel pleaded for an adjournment, but Shearn wanted to conclude the trial as quickly as possible, so he announced an evening session.

A Man Without a Soul-- That's Murderer Waite

The Waite case became big news around the United States. This sketch, made by an unknown artist working for the *Bismarck (ND) Daily Tribune*, shows three key figures in the case: Arthur Warren Waite, Percy Peck and Clara Waite. This sketch also appeared in the *Tacoma (WA) Times*. *From Chronicling America, Library of Congress.*

Following a ninety-minute break, the court would reconvene to hear the remainder of Waite's testimony. Women, Shearn said, would be excluded from the evening session.

At 8:00 p.m., Waite returned to the stand, where he would play to a considerably smaller audience.

Deuel resumed his questions about Waite's relationship with Catherine Peck.

She gave him many things, including diamonds, which Waite characterized as "outright gifts." Catherine, Waite said, gave him a large diamond ring, which he later slipped onto Clara's hand at the wedding under the pretense that he had purchased it with his life savings.

Aunt Catherine also gave him a ten-carat rock "as a keepsake," and "against her instructions," Waite took it to a jeweler, who cleaved the gemstone into pieces. He had one three-carat stone set into a ring and wore it about town before giving it to Margaret Horton when he said goodbye.

Deuel next questioned Waite about his attempts to murder his benefactor.

"Now in reference to Miss Catherine Peck, did you ever put ground glass in a can of marmalade?"

"I did, yes." Waite also admitted that during the summer of 1915—before his marriage to Clara—he spiked a can of fish with germ cultures obtained from human feces and gave it to Catherine Peck.

"And did you give her any other germs at any other time?"

"I gave her these others that I got from the laboratory." Waite said he mixed typhoid as well as other germs into Catherine's food. He explained that he obtained cultures of several very dangerous bacteria, including typhoid, diphtheria, pneumonia, influenza and streptococcus.

"Why did you want to grow bacteria and get them?" Deuel asked.

"Why?"

"Yes."

"Because I wanted to give them to these people."

"To what people?"

"To Miss [Catherine] Peck and Mrs. Peck and Mr. Peck."

Deuel wanted to drive home the idea of his client's depravity, so he asked Waite about a bizarre attempt to procure poison to put into Catherine Peck's tea. "Was there any arsenical fly paper in her room?"

"Oh, yes; I forgot about that. I had read somewhere about someone using fly paper which had some arsenic on it—the fly paper, it said, always did, and they soaked it and got the solution and then they would put it in the person's coffee. I read that in the paper a year ago or so; and so I got some fly paper and soaked it and then I took that and dried that, and I left some of the papers in her room so they would be found. But I guess I did not get enough, because it did not do anything."[171]

His attempts to murder Aunt Catherine, Waite explained, ended when Hannah Peck came to visit in January. He immediately seized the opportunity to begin poisoning her with diphtheria, typhoid and influenza germs he had acquired though William Webber. "And they acted on her immediately," Waite noted with a smile.

"Did you give her anything else besides germs?"

"I did, yes, sir. You see, she got sick and she got worse, but then she did not seem to get much worse; and so then I got some veronal." Just before midnight on January 29, he gave her the drugs. "I think I had a dozen tablets. And that was that night, you see—that Saturday night, maybe about eleven or twelve o'clock."

Waite paused and looked around the room. "And then I went to bed." The next morning, Clara discovered that her mother had died sometime that night.

"These dozens of germs that you gave Mrs. Peck, can you state whether there were millions or billions of these germs?"

Waite smiled. "Oh, well," he said nonchalantly, "billions—that is, there is no counting them, there would be so many."

The shocked jurors stared at Deuel, the *Sun* correspondent wrote, but then they fully realized the defense strategy. In the gallery sat "the alienists of the defense, Dr. Diefendorf and Dr. Karpas, industriously taking notes or making suggestions about questions."

At Deuel's prompting, Waite went on to detail his murder of John Peck. "And when Mr. Peck came, did you administer any [germs] to him?"

"Yes, I gave him better doses, but they did not affect him at all. And I kept giving him more bigger—very large doses, but they did not affect him." Waite said he gave John Peck the same "pathogenic" germs he gave Hannah Peck, including typhoid and diphtheria. "I got some tubercular sputum and put it in a syringe, a spray; and then I had him spray with that, when we would go out riding. He used the spray a good deal. And then I put this in instead of his regular spray. And then also later I put in the regular diphtheria and pneumonia organisms—into the spray."

This, Waite noted, did not work as intended. John Peck remained upright. He added, in a matter-of-fact tone, "and then I tried all the time to make them stronger—bigger doses and stronger, more virulent. But I could not get them strong enough; and so then I tried to make him weak and sick, and I got big doses of calomel—calomel tablets, you know, in the bottles—one grain and a half grain; and I would give him maybe half of a bottle at a time."

"How would you give it to him?"

"That I could put in any food, because I got these sweetened tablets, and you could put it on just where you could put sugar—it was white and powdered enough—it was white and rather sweet powder—so that it was not noticeable in the taste. And these would give the diarrhea that he had so severely."

Waite grinned in a way that made the *Sun* reporter cringe. "The man actually grinned," he wrote.[172]

Equally disgusted, the *New York Herald* reporter described Waite as acting like a comedian attempting to amuse the spectators. "Smirking whenever he related an especially repugnant or suggestive incident," he wrote, "he [Waite] grinned and glowed with seeming self-satisfaction."[173]

Deuel continued his questioning. "What other things did you try?"

Waite smiled. "Well, I was hoping to make the pneumococcus work, by giving him a cold; I would take him out riding in the automobile and leave the windows of the car all open on a cold night and drive all around; and then I would put water too on the sheets in his bed to make him catch cold."

Waite began to speak faster and in a slightly elevated tone as he progressed through his various attempts to murder John Peck.

"Did he catch cold?"

"No, he did not. And then I tried chlorine gas. I had read that the soldiers had got pneumonia after they had inhaled this gas—it makes the throat raw. And so I got some chlorine solution and put it in, but it did not work, it was too weak." Waite said that during a span of two weeks, he tried several other methods to murder John Peck, including feeding him large doses of calomel to weaken his system.

The calomel and the resultant diarrhea made Peck weak, Waite said, but not weak enough. He even seemed to improve slightly, and he planned to travel south to recuperate. Waite realized that he needed to work fast, so he purchased ninety grains of arsenic and began giving it to Peck on the Thursday or Friday before he died. He gave Peck a minute dose the first day, but he didn't become sick, so he gave him increasingly larger doses. By Saturday, March 11, Peck had ingested the entire ninety grains. He put the poison "in the food always—at some meal always."

Deuel asked Waite about the night John Peck died. "Describe in detail what you did after you went into his room that night."

"Well," Waite began, "he was quite in pain, and then it occurred to me—the doctor had said, I think, that hot soda was good to stop his pain and also aromatic spirits of ammonia; and we did not have any ammonia, but we had a little bottle of chloroform that Miss Catherine Peck had given to me quite a long time before for cleaning purposes." Waite said he went into the room and administered the chloroform until John Peck was unconscious. "And then finally I went into the hall and got a green pillow off the couch, because there was not, I thought, enough of the chloroform, and then I held the pillow tightly over his face."

Swann smiled. Waite had just confessed to smothering Peck, just as he theorized in his opening statement, even though his medical experts testified that the cause of death was arsenic poisoning.

The key point in Waite's testimony, as reporters pointed out in their day-after-trial coverage, came at about 10:00 p.m.

"What," Deuel asked, "was your purpose in administering germs to all these people?"

In a matter-of-fact tone, Waite described his reasons for obtaining virulent bacteria. "Well," he said, "because I wanted them to take sick and die."

"Why did you want them to die?"

"Because I wanted their money."

He wanted Catherine Peck to die first, he said, because her fortune would pass to John Peck. Then, when he dispatched John Peck, the sum total of the Peck fortune would pass in equal parts to Percy and Clara.

After prompting this stunning admission from Waite, Deuel had finished his questions, so Shearn decided to adjourn until the following morning.

<hr/>

The trial's fifth day—Friday, May 26, 1916—began with Waite back on the stand. Before Deuel handed him over to Brothers for what would surely be a grueling cross-examination, he asked one final sequence of questions.

"Dr. Waite, will you state whether or not you made any attempt to kill your wife?"

"I did not."

"Did you have the idea in your mind as to whether or not you would kill your wife?"

"I did have the idea for a time, but I am not sure whether I would have done so, and I made no attempt."

"No further questions, Your Honor." Deuel slumped into his chair. He was still exhausted from the marathon court session the night before.[174]

Brothers stood and took a deep breath. He needed to smash Waite's feeble attempt at a half-baked insanity defense. In addition to the twelve men in the jury box, he had to convince the alienists in the audience. He found himself in an unfamiliar position. As a prosecutor, he usually tried to underscore a defendant's depravity for the jury, but since Deuel's strategy was to prove Waite's behavior was so depraved that no sane man would act that way, Brothers would have to create the impression that Waite wasn't as wicked as he appeared to be.

Brothers began by grilling Waite about various statements he had made to Swann, Cunniff and others. Waite, however, had developed amnesia about these points. He didn't remember telling Detective Cunniff that he had purchased arsenic at John Peck's request. He didn't remember trying to finger Percy for the murder when he first met with Swann, and he didn't remember blaming "the man from Egypt." Brothers asked him twice more about "the man from Egypt," but both times, Waite denied ever mentioning the entity.

After a few more questions and a few more denials from the witness stand, Brothers turned to Waite's alleged depravity. "Haven't you been advised that if you went on this witness stand and made yourself out a notorious criminal that there would be at least one juror in this box who would think you were crazy?"

"I have not," Waite replied as if offended by the notion.

"And isn't that your hope?"

"That isn't my hope."

"Are you crazy?"

"I think not."

"And you wrote and signed a confession in Bellevue in which you stated you knew you deserved the penalty of death and were prepared to pay that penalty?" Brothers asked, referring to Waite's letter to the *World*.

"I am prepared."

Next, Brothers questioned the extent of Waite's plot.

"Isn't it a fact that you never took one single step towards taking the life of Catherine Peck?"

"It is not a fact that I never took one single step toward it."

"Yes," Brothers said.

"That is not a fact," Waite insisted.

"And that you never had in your hands any living bacteria of any time before you were married?"

Once again, Waite denied it. "That is not a fact."

Brothers quizzed Waite on his plot to murder Peck to obtain his fortune. Waite admitted to planning the murder as early as the summer of 1915.

"And when you succeeded in getting your hands upon the Peck money, you were going to leave the country?"

"That I cannot say."

"You and Margaret Horton were going away together?"

"We were not," Waite insisted.

After a few more questions, Brothers ended his cross with the clincher: "And there cannot be now, nor at any time, any doubt in any man's mind that you are guilty of this crime?"

"Not the slightest."

Brothers stared at Waite for a few seconds before returning to his chair.[175] Deuel needed to do a little damage control, so he reexamined Waite, focusing on his lapses of memory. Again, Waite denied remembering, among other things, the man from Egypt. After this line of questions, Waite was excused. He stepped down and trudged back to his chair. The spring in his step was gone.[176]

Catherine A. Peck, whom the press described as "a pleasant-faced woman," took the stand after the man who had tried to murder her. Since Brothers tried to establish that Waite's attempted murder of Catherine Peck was a work of fiction, Deuel wanted to corroborate statements Waite made on the witness stand, particularly the "marmalade incident."

"I bought this jar of orange marmalade," Catherine Peck explained, "the Dundee brand, and I took it home and ate part of it, and it appeared to be—that is, to my mind, full of sand." She also described the can of fish that Waite said he contaminated with feces. "It was not edible at all," she said.[177]

"Dr. Morris J. Karpas," William Penney bellowed.

Deuel hoped that Dr. Karpas would be one of two experts whose testimony would convince the jurors that Waite was mentally ill. An expert in "nervous and mental diseases," Dr. Karpas had interviewed Waite several times after his arrest. He found Waite tight-lipped until authorities transferred him to the Tombs; then Waite opened up about his crimes. According to Dr. Karpas, Waite admitted plotting the murders of Hannah and John Peck before his marriage to Clara. He also planned on killing Clara.[178]

Waite glanced at the courtroom ceiling like a bored student. Warren Waite didn't share his son's indifference. Tears streamed down his face as he listened to Dr. Karpas discuss his son's depravity.

Waite, Dr. Karpas testified, openly laughed when he described his attempts to murder Catherine Peck. When he detailed his various attempts to murder John Peck, he did it with frankness and without a hint of emotion. "[A]t this examination, the lack of moral sense was very striking," Dr. Karpas said. "There was no feeling whatever, particularly when he discussed his crime."[179]

Shearn interrupted Dr. Karpas's narrative to adjourn court for the noon recess.

At 2:00 p.m., Dr. Karpas returned to the stand to hear Deuel's five-thousand-word hypothetical question. The question, which took Deuel thirty-five minutes to read, detailed all of Waite's alleged wrongdoing going back to his childhood. Deuel had an ulterior motive; he wanted to catalogue Waite's numerous indiscretions for the jury. The underlying question, buried in layers of alleged wrongdoing, was simple: was Arthur Warren Waite of sound mind, and if not, what ailed him?

"He was suffering from moral imbecility," Dr. Karpas explained, "or otherwise known as moral insanity, or, by still others, moral idiocy—all synonymous for the same disease." He defined "moral imbecility" as "an abnormal mental condition characterized by lack of willpower and lack of feeling," which, he noted, was "a congenital condition."[180]

Brothers cross-examined Dr. Karpas. He began by asking Dr. Karpas to detail his experience with examining murderers. Karpas admitted that Waite was the first criminal he had formally examined, although he had seen two other criminals in Bellevue.

Brothers then rattled off a sequence of questions about Waite's attempts to cover his tracks and his evident motive—money—but Dr. Karpas stuck to his diagnosis. All of Waite's actions, he believed, could be seen as those of a man with a warped mentality. He didn't want Waite to go free but felt that Waite needed to go to Matteawan, not Sing Sing.[181]

Penney summoned Deuel's second mental health expert, Dr. Allen R. Dieffendorf.

Like his colleague, Dr. Dieffendorf visited Waite in the Tombs and listened to a few shocking admissions. Waite said after Hannah Peck's death, he rifled through the clothes on her body and stole eighty dollars. He also said his interest in medicine was for the sole purpose of completing his scheme of murdering the Pecks. Each time Waite had admitted to something shocking, Dr. Dieffendorf said, he laughed heartily.

After three interviews with Waite, Dieffendorf arrived at the same conclusion as his colleague: Waite suffered from moral imbecility. "It seemed to me that he was entirely devoid of emotions or feeling," he said.[182]

When Dr. Dieffendorf left the stand, court was adjourned for the day. It was a fortuitous break for Deuel; the last thing the jury heard was the insistence of his experts that Waite lacked the moral sense of a "normal" man.

14

VERDICT

NEW YORK, NEW YORK

Saturday, May 27, 1916

The psychological debate continued on Saturday morning when Swann called three rebuttal witnesses: mental health experts Dr. Smith Ely Jelliffe, Dr. William Mabon and Dr. Menas Gregory.

Waite, according to Dr. Jelliffe, "was a great deal of a poseur," who "would distinctly endeavor to fabricate, or to exaggerate, and endeavor to mislead" throughout his examinations. Waite didn't want to acknowledge the enormity of the trouble he was in, but this was characteristic of others in the same boat. "In my opinion, he was sane," Dr. Jelliffe concluded.[183]

Dr. William Mabon followed his colleague to the stand and testified about the four interviews he conducted with Waite. Like Jelliffe, he saw nothing that convinced him the defendant was anything other than sane. When Deuel asked him about Waite's affect during the trial—his constant smiling while on the witness stand—Mabon said he thought Waite was putting on a show.

For his last expert witness, Brothers called Dr. Gregory, supervisor of Bellevue Hospital's "psychopathic, alcoholic and prison services." Like Dieffendorf and Mabon, Dr. Gregory concluded that Waite was sane and well aware of the consequences of his actions when he murdered John Peck. He also believed that Waite was attempting to fake insanity. During Deuel's brief cross, however, Dr. Gregory characterized Waite as a "born criminal" who had a faulty moral sense.

After Deuel finished his cross of Dr. Gregory, he returned to his table, took a long sip from a glass of water and approached the jury box to begin his closing argument.

Walter Deuel's remarks consumed forty minutes. He characterized the conflicting testimony of the alienists as "a crisis" but suggested that no man who did what Waite admitted to doing could be considered sane. "As to his moral sense," he asked, "how can anybody do the things that he did, do the repeated acts that he did, looking to kill a human being and have any moral sense whatsoever—any idea as to his duties toward society?"

Would a man with "moral sense" put water in John Peck's rubbers and dampen his bedsheets in an attempt to weaken his immune system so the germs would work more efficiently? Would such a man administer ninety grains of arsenic when a fatal dose was two and a half to four? If Waite was sane, Deuel pointed out, then why would he do things like sign the poison register in his own name? "Is there any coordination of thought in a mind that will operate like that?"

And then, Deuel noted, there was his affect on the stand—smiling when he described unthinkable acts like inducing diarrhea with heavy doses of calomel, chloroforming and then smothering Peck with a pillow.

Deuel ended with one final plea: "Would you have it upon your conscience to send an idiot to the chair, a person without understanding whatsoever, a lunatic, a child of tender years? I think not." Deuel returned to his chair and watched as Brothers began his concluding argument.[184]

George Brothers walked over to the jury box, leaned on the rail and began his closing remarks. He characterized Waite as a man trapped by the overwhelming evidence of his guilt and who turned to an insanity plea as a last resort.

"This defendant says himself he was not insane," Brothers pointed out, "that he never was insane." He scanned the faces of the jurors. "However, two other individuals have come temporarily from their obscure positions, and come here before you gentlemen in a vain attempt to put something over," Brothers said, implying that Deuel had treated them like fools.

Waite's premeditation, Brothers said, was evident in the details. The murder took place on a Sunday, when Waite knew that all official government departments—including the DA's office—would be closed. Both Hannah and John Peck died "in the middle of the night," and their bodies were taken from the city on Sunday afternoon.

Then, Brothers noted, there were Waite's many attempts to cover up his crime: the attempted cremation, the alleged $25,000 bribe to Kane and a Machiavellian maneuver to visit Swann's office to offer his help and thus throw off any suspicion of him. "Does an innocent man prepare a defense before he is accused?" Brothers asked, pausing for the jurors to think about the statement.

Father Hans B. Schmidt, a priest who clandestinely married housekeeper Anna Aumüller in New York City. When he discovered she was pregnant, he slit her throat. Despite an attempt to feign insanity during his subsequent trial, a jury convicted him of first-degree murder. He died in Sing Sing's electric chair on February 18, 1916. Newspapers covering the Waite case often compared Waite's insanity defense with that of Schmidt. *From the Bain News Service, Library of Congress.*

Opposite: Anna Aumüller, circa 1913. *From the Bain News Service, Library of Congress.*

The Bridge of Sighs, circa 1905. Waite passed across this bridge from his cell in the Tombs to the criminal courts building, where his trial took place. *From the Detroit Publishing Company, Library of Congress.*

Waite, Brothers noted, then tried to take the coward's way out of his fix, "and that poor little woman, Mrs. Horton, whom this defendant, by his devilish wiles and ingenuity, tempted away from her own home, and probably has ruined her life, was the one that he got to go and buy the poison with which to take his life. He could buy poison for the Pecks but not for himself. This alone is positive proof that this defendant had a full realization that he had committed crime." Brothers smiled. "Suicide is confession of guilt," he said.

Brothers looked at Waite, who smirked. Disgusted, Brothers pointed to the defendant. "The same smile, gentlemen, that won Mr. Peck and Mrs. Peck and Aunt Kate and all his friends and acquaintances. It is the friend that got him out of trouble in South Africa and Mackinac Island. Shall a smile be a defense? Shall we turn loose this moral pestilence upon the streets again because of a smile?" Brothers asked in concluding.[185]

In his lengthy remarks to the jury, Justice Shearn addressed the notion of "moral imbecility."

"Gentlemen of the jury: No such plea as 'moral imbecility' is admissible under our law. It may be well known in medicine, but it is not known to the law." The idea of "moral depravity as a defense," Shearn explained, had been recently debated by the Court of Appeals in the Hans Schmidt case and rejected. Shearn read a relevant portion of the court's decision.[186]

After his instructions, at about 1:20 p.m., Justice Shearn sent the jurors off to deliberate.

Meanwhile, officers escorted Waite across the Bridge of Sighs to the Tombs, where he awaited the verdict in his cell, number 138. He chomped down a piece of chocolate cake, quaffed down a mug of coffee and whistled a few tunes before striking up a conversation with a fellow inmate.

Frank Waite waited with his brother. "Maybe they will find you not guilty," he said, although the flat tone of his statement belied his true belief about the verdict.

"No," Arthur said without emotion. "I'm guilty."[187]

Just a little over an hour later, Waite received word: after only eighty-three minutes, including a break for lunch, the jury had reached a verdict.

⟫•◦•⟪

At 2:45 p.m., a crowd of curious news reporters, including Robert Rohde, gathered in Justice Shearn's courtroom to witness the climax of Waite's historic trial. From jury selection to verdict, the trial consumed only five days—a dubious record in the lengthy annals of New York City crime. The

1892 trial of Carlyle Harris, who fed his wife an overdose of morphine, lasted fourteen days. The 1912 trial of Charles Becker, the New York cop who faced a jury for murdering a gambler, took sixteen days.[188]

Rohde watched as Arthur Warren Waite walked into the courtroom. It was the closest Rohde, or any other member of the press, had come to the defendant since the trial began.

During the trial, Dr. Waite had simply stopped speaking to reporters. Correspondents from every major newspaper sent notes requesting interviews, but everyone received a curt reply: "Nothing to say." Waite's tight lips prompted Rohde to characterize him as one of "the most ungettable prisoners the Tombs ever held." Rohde wanted to inspect some of the poetry Waite had authored while in jail, but like the others, Waite just turned him away.

Then, just before Waite walked back across the Bridge of Sighs to hear the jury's verdict, he jotted a quick note and asked Deuel to deliver it to the herd of reporters that was gathering at the courthouse. He would not sit for interviews at the time, Waite explained in the note, but he was writing down "his impressions" and would perhaps speak to them later.

For Rohde, this enigmatic statement explained why Waite had suddenly and inexplicably stopped talking to the press. "It was one way of serving notice," Rohde later explained, "that the days of free copy provided by Arthur Warren Waite were over—an invitation for bids."[189] Waite, it appeared, would make one last attempt to profit from his scheme.

With a spring in his step, Waite walked past his father, who sat in the gallery next to his other two sons, Frank and Clyde. He took his seat next to Crater and Deuel.

"Will the prisoner please stand?" William Penney commanded. Waite stood, emotionless, and stared at the floor. "Gentlemen of the jury," Penney asked, "have you agreed upon a verdict?"

Jury foreman Robert Neill stood, straightened his jacket and said, "Yes."

"What say you, gentlemen, is the defendant guilty or not guilty?"

"Guilty as charged," Neill said.[190]

Clara Louise Peck fainted. Warren Waite buried his face in his hands and began to sob, tears running down his cheeks. But Arthur remained apparently unaffected. The word "guilty," a *New York Tribune* writer commented, had no more effect on Waite's emotions than "a pin prick on the skin of a side show ossified man."[191]

As Waite left the packed courtroom, he was still smiling but paler in complexion. He shuffled past his father and brothers without so much as glancing at them.

Warren Waite virtually collapsed. He leaned on Frank's arm as they left the courtroom. "What can I say? What can I say? My heart is broken," he uttered as he hobbled past the *Sun* correspondent.[192]

Clara Peck couldn't quite avoid the reporters, who raced over to her as soon as Waite was escorted from the court back to his Tombs cell. She stated, "You must excuse me. I have no desire to discuss the verdict, except to say it is awful."

George Brothers, standing next to Clara, characterized the verdict as the only logical decision. "The evidence was overwhelming," he commented.

With a hint of sarcasm in his voice, Walter Deuel gave a brief statement. "As long as the jury would not take into consideration our plea of insanity," Deuel said, "it was a fair verdict. Under the statutes, the verdict was just and proper."[193]

Swann, reticent of the press, uttered a solitary line: "The jury has said the last word."[194]

After the trial, a *New York Tribune* writer cornered one of the jurors, who described the deliberations. "When he smiled on the stand, Waite signed his own death warrant. Coupled with the horrible story he was reciting to us, it was ghastly," the unnamed juror explained. "Waite used to make friends with that smile. We in the jury box knew why he was smiling. He was looking for sympathy, trying to persuade some single one of us to hold out against the chair. That had been his game from the first."

In the end, concluded the *Tribune* writer, it wasn't the mass of evidence presented by the prosecution that damned Waite, "it was the dentist's own friendly grin which convicted him."[195]

By Thursday morning, June 1, 1916, Arthur Warren Waite had become irritated with the restrictions that prison authorities had placed on him. The better part of the week had passed as he awaited sentencing, scheduled for later that morning.

He leered at the guard as he slurped his breakfast with a spoon.

"I understand that you have a triple guard watching me," he growled as he noticed Tombs warden John Hanley approach his cell. "It isn't necessary. I will do nothing to commit suicide. I won't even make an attempt upon my life. It is perfectly safe to let me have a knife and fork with my food instead of making me eat with a spoon."[196] He had endured such restrictions for three days.

Hanley smirked, which irritated Waite, but he knew that he had spent his last night in the Tombs. Later that morning, the court would go through the formality of sentencing. Afterward, he expected, they would transport him to Sing Sing's death house.

In his Tombs cell, Waite had tried to maintain his bravado throughout the week, but his façade had begun to crack. While Waite always grinned around others, the guards noticed behavior that suggested he wasn't as calm as he seemed. More and more he read from the Bible, penciled passages from it onto notebook paper and refused to speak to reporters. Instead, he had issued a brief public statement. "I don't want to see anyone," Waite said. "I want to be left alone with my Bible. From now until the day I go into the chair I will devote myself to my Bible."[197]

The pressure was clearly getting to Arthur Warren Waite.

Fearing that Waite might try to cheat the hangman, Tombs authorities had taken precautions. On Monday morning, they took away his knife and fork, which led to a false rumor that Waite had tried to kill himself.[198]

After breakfast, Waite broke his official silence. Just before crossing the Bridge of Sighs for sentencing, he issued a formal statement to the press.

"I want to go to Sing Sing as soon as I can, the sooner the better. I am not looking for sympathy. I am guilty, and the public knows it. I reiterate that I want no appeal from the verdict the jury made for me. I wish that Thursday was here now, so that the formality of sentencing would be over. I don't want anyone to be sorry for me. I am ready to pay with my own life for the one I took. I knew what I did when I killed Mr. Peck and I am ready to pay the penalty, the sooner the better."[199]

Waite also said he wanted nothing to do with an appeal. "[It] would simply mean a prolongation of an unpardonable crime. The first time I see my attorney I will instruct him not to take an appeal."

He then addressed the ultimate punishment: "I have done wrong and should be punished for it. I am anxious to go to the chair. I will go with my head erect and will not flinch from the penalty the law justly prescribes for such a crime as I committed."[200]

⎯⎯►•◄⎯⎯

The sentencing was short and to the point. Waite sat and listened as Deuel made several futile motions, which took Shearn mere seconds to deny. As William Penney instructed, the now-convicted slayer stood to hear the court's sentencing.

Sing Sing prison, circa 1915. *From the Bain News Service, Library of Congress.*

"Arthur Warren Waite, indicted as Arthur W. Waite," Penney asked, "have you any legal cause to show why judgment of death should not now be pronounced against you?"

Waite looked at Justice Shearn. "May I say a few words, Your Honor?"

"Yes," Shearn responded.

Waite praised the court, his counsel Walter Deuel and even George Brothers for the "conscientiousness" with which he did "his duty by society" in prosecuting the case. "And then I would like to say, if I may," Waite added, "that I cannot undo the wrong that I have done. I realize fully what it is. To some of the people the wrong is far beyond asking forgiveness. That would be humanly impossible. I simply would like to say that I am glad, very glad, to give my body in expiation, if it may, in any small degree, make up or rectify in their minds that hurt which I have done them."

Waite looked around the courtroom and smiled. He remembered a favorite strategy of stage actors, a pause before delivering a key line. "I only wish I had more than one body to give, and I hope that my soul may go on and serve hereafter those whom I injured. If there be any whom I have not so grievously injured, I hope that they will forgive me. I am thoroughly sorry. I thank you. That is all."[201]

Shearn ordered Waite to be held in solitary confinement in Sing Sing's death house and set the execution date. Arthur Warren Waite would take the long walk to Sing Sing's hot seat sometime during the week of July 10, 1916.

PRISONER NO. 67281

SING SING DEATH HOUSE, OSSINING, NEW YORK

Sunday, June 11, 1916–Friday, May 18, 1917

On Sunday, June 11, 1916, Prisoner No. 67281 made a surprise appearance in print. Since his transfer to Sing Sing's death house, Waite was off-limits to the press, but just before he left the Tombs, he became the unlikely victim of a reporter's trick. Robert Rohde had finally finagled a meeting with the convicted slayer after duping the con man. He sent a note hinting "that the prison poet probably would be richer when we parted, once we ever met." Rohde hoped the promise of a payday would coax Waite into agreeing to meet the reporter. "It worked like a charm," Rohde later commented.[202]

Hooked, Waite immediately replied: "Come up and we'll talk." The interview, conducted in Waite's cell at the Tombs, made it into print in mid-June, almost two weeks after Waite's transfer to the big house. The timing was strategic. Prison authorities did not allow the media access to death-row inmates, so Rohde's interview would be the only such article published during Waite's incarceration in Sing Sing.

Waite had continued to fascinate and confound the public as he whiled away the days until the appeals court considered Deuel's appeal of the case. Walter Deuel hadn't followed Waite's instructions; after sentencing, he immediately began the appeals process, which caused an indeterminate delay in Waite's execution date. In the interim, Waite arrived at Sing Sing on June 1, handcuffed to fellow inmate Leo James, a thief beginning an eighteen-month sentence.

An *Evening Telegram* reporter rode along in the car that transported Waite from the Ossining train station to the prison and jotted down every word the prisoner uttered on the short trip.

Still smiling, slightly: photograph taken while Waite was Inmate 67281 of Sing Sing. *Photograph of Arthur W. Waite, Crime in New York, 1850–1950 Image Collection, Lewis Lawes Collection, Special Collections, Lloyd Sealy Library, John Jay College of Criminal Justice.*

"I have no sympathy for my victims, and I want no sympathy for myself. Money was my curse and was the thing which led to my crimes. I have no excuses to make," Waite said with no inflection in his voice.

Shocked by this apparent lack of feeling, the reporter asked Waite if he was touched that Clara fainted when the jury foreman read the verdict of "guilty."

"She had no reason to faint," he said flatly, and repeated his assertion that he was ready to die for his crimes.[203]

As Waite settled in his death house cell, he learned that two of the eighteen men would go to the chair the next day. "I wish I was, too," he remarked.[204]

The morning after Waite arrived at the death house, Roy Champlain and Giovanni Supe took the long walk. The double execution unhinged Oresto Shillitoni, awaiting his turn in the chair following a conviction for three counts of murder. Shillitoni ransacked his cell and caused such a ruckus that Waite yelled for the guards. "Take the man out," he screamed. "He's crazy!"[205]

For Waite, the time couldn't go fast enough. While Deuel did his best to keep his client from la chaise, Waite killed time by reading and writing. He was particularly fascinated by English romantics such as Keats and Shelley and jotted out his own verse on sheets of lined paper.

Robert Rohde's interview with Waite provided readers with a rare glimpse at the condemned prisoner's mindset. Waite had greeted Rohde with a warm handshake and flashed what by now had become his signature grin—the same expression he wore when he confessed to poisoning John E. Peck.

The "rhyming dentist" had impressed Rohde: "Waite looked as if he had stepped from under a shower five minutes before. He was clean-shaved and immaculate of linen; his shoes were shined and his trousers pressed."

"I managed to keep fairly fresh," Waite explained. "That's because, half the time, I'm wandering in fields and woods. They can keep my body here in prison, but my spirit slips through the bars at will. When I'm writing my poetry I'm no more among these criminals…" Waite paused.

"About the poetry?" Rohde asked.

"Oh yes. I'm awfully glad you're interested in it. That's what I want to do—leave something behind so that people won't remember me just by the bad things I've done. I don't think of any better way to spend what's left of my life than in writing little poems."

Waite characterized his poetry as "mystical," as how he could be "here in body and roaming in the fields at the same time; why, I don't worry any more about the electric chair than I did before I had any thought of sitting in it."

When Rohde asked to see some of Waite's "mystical" text, Waite said that he didn't have any of it with him. Waite, the consummate con man, had pulled a fast one on Rohde. "My brother," he explained, "has every last bit of it."[206]

Waite shocked Rohde when he said he wasn't "money mad."

"I'm not," Waite insisted, "and it isn't fair to infer it. Money doesn't mean a thing to me, now. Those days have passed. Once I wanted all the dollars I could get my hands on. I gambled for them and I lost. Now I'm just waiting to pay the score. But I don't see any reason—do you?—why I shouldn't be earning something as I wait."

Waite explained his motive for murdering the Pecks. "They were getting old and had a fortune. I was young, but getting older, and there was danger I

[O, let my lesson hearts instruct]

Arthur Warren Waite, 1916

O, let my lesson hearts instruct,
That mild and sweet their days may wrap them round;
That from my failure God may now construct
Those vessels shapelier than they'd else be found.

I wait the close of day with outstretched arms,
I long to turn again into the dark;
While here my actions others' progress harms.
But footprints left are seen and men will mark.

As gently down into the lake's calm blue
One steps and pauses at the little chill,
And then moves on and only leaves a few
Small ripples circling far and further still.

So gently moves the image into death.
Its passing scarce of note grows less and less.
And all is Dark—except the Living Breath
Unseen to eyes is freed from its distress.

Perhaps the Breath lent me has served God well,
For some must show the false compared to true,
And, too, perhaps that's why I heard Him tell
That in that Breath I found my own life too.

My own life found—and may it live through Death
To fall in humble servitude before
Those souls whose wrongs are righted by that Breath
Which gives and takes—and bolts the little door.

This selection of Waite's prison poetry is supposedly biographical and was one of two pieces published in the June 12, 1916 edition of the *Sun*. The "little door" may represent the "little green door" of Sing Sing's death house.

should be too old to enjoy the money to the full when it came into my hands. A few years of life, more or less, would mean nothing to them, yet those few years might be made into the happiest of my life. So I did what I did."

After briefly discussing his crimes, Waite returned to his literary musings and suggested Rohde contact Frank Waite to see the poems. Rohde asked Waite if he had any desire to write a memoir, but Waite said it would be a laborious undertaking.

Waite thought for a moment about the possibility of a prison memoir and asked Rohde what newspapers paid fellows like him.

Rohde shrugged and said he made just enough to pay "the rent of five rooms in Flatbush."

Waite frowned. He thought for a few seconds. "Yes, but you haven't killed a couple of people. That's probably all you're worth to the man who's paying you. If you ever get where I am, then, probably, you'll be able to command as much as I'll get, or even more."[207]

After haggling over the potential price of a nonexistent work, Rohde left without the poems he wanted, but he didn't leave empty-handed either. The interview appeared as a feature article in the Sunday, June 11, 1916 edition of the *New York Tribune* entitled "Peddling Poems from the Death House."

Rohde didn't acquire any of Waite's poetry, but the world would not be robbed. Of the fifty poems Waite penned in prison, which he sent to Frank in a sealed envelope, a few leaked to the press. Warden Kirchwey, however, was not amused. Believing it was an attempt to drum up support for the condemned man, he jailed Waite's "poetic muse" when he forbade any more poems from leaving the death house.

<hr />

It was a crisp fall morning on October 16, 1916, when former Sing Sing warden Thomas Mott Osborne greeted the *Daily Standard Union* reporter with a firm handshake. Osborne was as close as the reporter—or any reporter—was going to get to Arthur Warren Waite.

Osborne had become warden in 1914, and in his desire to reform the prison, he lived among the population for a week. He became a tireless advocate of prison reform, but weary of the battle with state officials, he resigned in late 1916. During his last few months in charge of the prison, Osborne—considered a keen penologist with a sharp eye—came to know Arthur Warren Waite.[208]

Warden Thomas Mott Osborne among prisoners, circa 1915. A notable prison reformer and "penologist," Osborne famously spent time among the general population in order to identify areas in need of improvement. *From the Bain News Service, Library of Congress.*

Warden Osborne poses by a Sing Sing cell block, circa 1915. Osborne came to know Waite well during their brief association. *From the Bain News Service, Library of Congress.*

"Do you think that Dr. Arthur Warren Waite, who confessed to murdering his wife's parents, is a good man? Or is he bad; inherently criminal and vicious?" the *Daily Standard Union* correspondent asked.

"I think Dr. Waite is insane, not violently insane, but excessively abnormal. He has control over his mental processes, but his mind is so warped and distorted that his murdering his father- and mother-in-law by poison is not surprising."

Osborne paused as he waited for the reporter to take notes. After a few minutes, he continued. "I have studied Waite in the death house at Sing Sing. His predominant characteristics are excessive self-centering, utter selfishness and extreme sensuousness." Although Osborne—a death penalty opponent—felt Waite deserved life in prison, he did not believe he should go to the chair.

"What does he say about himself now that he has been in the death house for several months?" the journalist asked.

"He says what I very seriously doubt—that he has had a change of heart. He writes poetry. Oh, awful poetry. And he reads the Bible. Poor fellow. I think he is having a fine time. Just as he had them when he was racing up and down Broadway in an automobile and pretending to perform delicate operations at hospitals, he still has his feminine admirers and he revels in them just as much as ever." Osborne scratched his head. "You would be astounded at the number and sort of women who write to him. You should see the line of gush that some of them send him, to which he replies in kind. One woman has discovered that she is his soul mate!"

The reporter chuckled. Osborne leaned back in his chair and tucked his hands into his vest pockets.[209]

Waite looked down at a blank sheet of paper and scratched the date—Friday, May 18, 1917—at the top of the page. He sighed. Ten months had passed since the original scheduled date of his execution. Yet the question of his execution was no longer "if" but "when." Six weeks earlier, on April 3, the court had rejected his final appeal and ruled that his execution would take place sometime during the week of May 21. Impatient, Waite decided to ink a letter to Warden Moyer, requesting his execution take place on the earliest possible date in the allotted time frame, Monday, May 21.

He thought about his father, who couldn't stomach the idea of his son going to the chair. While awaiting Arthur's execution, Warren Waite's health went into decline. The fifty-nine-year-old died on March 23, 1917—exactly one year after news of John E. Peck's murder hit the front

Convicted slayer and former cop Charles Becker (center with "x" over his head) being escorted to Sing Sing. Jailers praised Becker for his iron nerve, but he broke down on the way to the chair in July 1915. Waite, according to Tombs warden John Hanley, displayed more nerve than Becker. *From the Bain News Service, Library of Congress.*

pages in Grand Rapids. The cause of death was recorded as pneumonia, but some speculated that he died of a broken heart.[210]

Waite returned to the blank sheet of paper and began his note.

To Warden Moyer:

Dear Sir: In one of the newspapers today is the statement (which you can verify) that "A.W. Waite is to die next week," and on inquiry I learn that you have the power to name the day of that week.

I am sure you would not be averse to obliging me if you found it possible and reasonable to do so, and I wonder if we could not arrange for the Monday of next week.

There really is a reason for asking this, although I will not trouble you with explanations.

I would be very grateful indeed for this favor. Yours respectfully,

Arthur Warren Waite[211]

Waite put down the pen and thought about Charles Becker, who went to the chair on the morning of July 30, 1915. Tombs warden John Hanley once praised Waite for having more nerve than Becker. Waite hoped his former jailer was right.

Known as a man of iron will, Becker broke down as two priests escorted him to the chair. He trembled as the executioners strapped him to the chair. His voice cracking, he uttered a final prayer: "Into thy hands, O Lord, I commend my spirit." As he said the word "spirit," the executioner threw the lever, and the force of 1,850 volts caused his body to jerk against the leather straps. It took three shocks to kill him.[212]

Moyer received Waite's sealed envelope that evening. He read the letter but didn't oblige Waite's request. He scheduled the execution for Thursday, May 24. Waite would have to wait almost another week.

THE LONG WALK

SING SING DEATH HOUSE, OSSINING, NEW YORK

Thursday, May 24, 1917

The day had finally come for Waite to give his "body in expiation" for the murder of John E. Peck. In the interim, reporters had chased other stories, but on the eve of Arthur's execution, Waite once again became front-page news. Most of the characters in the drama stayed away from Sing Sing, but they couldn't avoid Arthur Warren Waite altogether, as reporters hounded them for their thoughts.

Percy Peck planned to visit Waite before the execution but changed his mind and remained in Grand Rapids. He did not have mercy on his mind when he described his thought process to a reporter. "I wanted to see him and thought it would make his punishment all the more bitter. But I decided not to. I guess he will suffer enough as it is."[213]

Clara Peck also remained in Grand Rapids. She told a friend, who in turn relayed the conversation to a reporter, that she hoped Arthur's sentence would be commuted. Regardless, she said, "I will feel freer when it is all over."[214]

Friends and family shooed nosy reporters away from the Waite residence in Grand Rapids, where Sarah Waite devoted the afternoon of Thursday, May 24, to reading the Bible. In the months between Warren's death and her son's execution, her health had rapidly deteriorated. Many of her closest friends and relatives doubted she would recover and predicted she wouldn't outlive her son by long.

A *Syracuse Daily Journal* writer characterized Warren and Sarah Waite as unintentional victims of their son's poison plot. "His mother is dying from grief at her home in Grand Rapids. His father died of a broken heart a month ago. His brother, Frank, his only loyal friend throughout, has turned snowy haired in less than a year over his brother's conduct."[215]

Margaret Horton was newsworthy only in her conspicuous absence. The woman who had remained loyal to Waite had simply dropped out of the limelight, apparently abandoning her Romeo to his fate. She refused to visit Waite in Sing Sing and avoided newspapermen as if they had a virulent disease.

<hr>

On the morning of Waite's execution, guards roused him out of a deep slumber at 8:00 a.m. They moved him to one of the older death-row cells, just a few strides away from the green door. The prison barber gave him a quick trim, and a guard hung a new set of clothes by the prison bars.

As Waite consumed a light breakfast of bacon and eggs, a bowl of cereal, some fruit and a strong cup of coffee, the electrician walked past and disappeared through the green door. A few seconds later, the lights dimmed as the electrician tested the current.

Just after noon, the prison physician, Dr. Amos O. Squire, visited Waite. Squire checked his pulse and was astonished to learn that it was completely normal. He had followed this routine physical for dozens of men who had died in the electric chair, and in every case, they displayed elevated blood pressure. But Waite appeared as calm as a man about to take a leisurely walk in the park.

That afternoon, Frank Waite went to see his baby brother for the last time. Waite dined on a light supper of eggs and toast while the brothers chatted about the old days when they spent hours tobogganing down the gentle slope that ran from their neighborhood to the edge of the Grand River.

When he stood up to leave, Frank broke down and began to sob. "I'm going now, Arthur. Goodbye," he managed to utter. He took a few gasps. After a few seconds, he regained his composure. "Is there any message—anything I can tell anybody—anything?"

Arthur shook his head. "Goodbye, Frank. Don't worry for me. I shall not suffer. There is no message to anybody."[216] He reached out and grasped Frank's hand, shaking it like a man who had just sealed a business deal. Frank Waite darted out of Sing Sing with tears streaming down his cheeks.

After his brother left, Waite spent much of the evening on the literary pursuits he had developed during his incarceration. He read poems by Keats and attempted to pen one of his own but couldn't manage to finish it. Instead, he wrote a note to Dr. Squire, folded it and slipped it inside an envelope. He scribbled "May 19, Private" on the front of the envelope and sealed it. He placed the envelope inside a second envelope, sealed it and scrawled "to be opened after my death" across the front.

As the fatal hour approached, Waite felt conflicting emotions. It couldn't come fast enough, yet he hoped time would slow down. He flinched as his cell door opened with a metallic shriek at about 9:00 p.m. As Waite noticed the familiar figure of Dr. A.N. Peterson, the prison chaplain, standing at the cell door, he felt weak in the knees and became aware of a slight trembling in his hands. Despite his desire to expedite his own execution, Waite felt his pulse beating in his neck. He was terrified. Nevertheless, he managed a smile as the chaplain entered his cell.

Peterson and Waite spent the next two hours in prayer. As the hour hand neared eleven, Peterson asked Waite if he could deliver any last messages. "Arthur, is there any message you want to send to anybody?"

"No, thank you, Doctor, I have nothing to say to anyone on this earth."

"But your mother—"

Waite interrupted Peterson. "To nobody on this earth," he repeated in a slow, firm tone. "Frank told me about mother's illness, but it is not as bad as reported. I have nothing to say to her."[217]

Just before 11:00 p.m., Warden Moyer appeared and asked Waite if he had any last statement he wished to make. Waite shook his head and turned to Fred Dorner, the head keeper in charge of death row. "Well, Mr. Dorner, are you ready? Is it time?" Waite asked as he stood up. He followed Dorner and Dr. Peterson out of the cell. He felt his knees buckle slightly but took a deep breath, which seemed to temporarily steel his nerves.

As Dorner escorted Waite through the death house with Dr. Peterson following on their heels, Waite's death-row neighbors stood at their cell doors to say farewell. Three of them whispered, "Goodbye, Arthur," in hushed tones through the black curtains traditionally hung over the death-row cells on the date of an execution.

"Goodbye, boys," Waite remarked with his best attempt at a cavalier, nonchalant tone of voice. "God bless you."

At 11:03 p.m., Waite passed through the infamous "green door," which long before had faded to a burnt brown color. A small group of reporters and witnesses watched as prisoner No. 67281 shuffled into the execution chamber. The color drained from his face as he eyed the chair.

Once again, Waite put on a stoic façade. "Is this all there is to it?" he asked and threw a quick smile at the witnesses that seemed eerily familiar to the *New*

Sing Sing's electric chair, circa 1915. The "little green door" leading to the death house cells is at the right. *From the Library of Congress.*

York Times correspondent. "Waite," he noticed, "wore to death the same grin that marked him when he made his confession upon the witness stand a year ago."[218]

Waite felt his knees grow weak, but he didn't lose his nerve. He stared at the floor, walked straight to the chair and fell into the hot seat.

Dr. Peterson opened his Bible to the bookmarked page and began reading the twenty-third Psalm as two guards wearing blue uniforms began fastening Waite's arms and legs to the chair. They tossed a black leather strap across Waite's knees, pulled it taut and buckled it. They repeated the procedure, fastening a strap across Waite's ankles, another across his wrists and then another across his chest.

"The Lord is my shepherd," Peterson began, "I shall not want. He maketh me lie down in green pastures; he leadeth me beside the still waters."

Waite focused on the prayer as the attendants finished pinioning him. They slipped a black leather cap over his head, fastened a leather strap across his forehead that covered his eyes and attached the electrodes to his temples. They worked fast. The entire process took just two minutes.

"Surely goodness and mercy shall follow me all the days of my life, and I will dwell in the house of the Lord forever." Dr. Peterson paused and closed his Bible.

At 11:05 p.m., Warden Moyer asked Waite if he had any last words, but he had nothing more to say.[219]

Dr. Squire nodded, and one of the guards threw a switch that sent two thousand volts surging into Waite's body.

Waite's body jerked against the straps, and a sickly sweet odor of burning flesh began to fill the chamber. The initial blast lasted for a minute and fifteen seconds.

Dr. Squire leaned down and placed his stethoscope against Waite's chest. He heard a slight murmur, so he stepped back and gave the signal for a second blast. Once again, the attendant threw the switch, sending another wave of two thousand volts into Waite's body at 11:08 p.m.

After the second five-second jolt, Dr. Squire placed his stethoscope against Waite's chest. This time, he heard nothing but silence. At 11:11 p.m., he pronounced Arthur Warren Waite dead. Dr. Perry M. Townsend, a New York physician on hand to assist Dr. Squire, concurred.

The *New York Times* correspondent who witnessed the execution provided a fitting epitaph in the paper's May 25 edition: "2,000 volts ended the life of one of the most remarkable individuals in criminal history."[220]

Back in his office, Dr. Amos Squire opened the envelope Waite had left for him. Inside was a solitary sheet of paper containing a single statement, a quote from a letter by Robert Louis Stevenson: "Call us with morning faces, eager to labour, eager to be happy—Stevenson."[221]

In the days following Waite's execution, people and the press alike continued to speculate about his mental state. The *Day Book*—a periodical published in Chicago—ran an item under the title "Are Eyes of 2 Insanity Pleaders Alike?" Below the headline were close-ups showing the eyes of Waite and Harry Thaw, who infamously murdered architect Stanford White over a beauty named Evelyn Nesbitt. Like Waite, Thaw tried an insanity gambit, but unlike Waite, it worked; the jury found him criminally insane, and the court sentenced him to a stint in Matteawan.

The *Day Book* writer found a clue in the eyes of the two villains. "Alienists generally agree," the *Day Book* writer noted, "that in insane persons more of the whites of the eyes are visible than in those of normal mind. Thaw's large,

Harry K. Thaw, who murdered wealthy New York architect Stanford White. Newspaper reporters didn't fail to miss several parallels between Thaw and Waite. Both enjoyed playboy lifestyles. Thaw, like Waite, fell for a chorus girl after watching her perform. After the first trial ended in deadlock, the jury at Thaw's second trial found him not guilty by reason of insanity. He was sentenced to life at Matteawan State Hospital for the criminally insane. Following a third trial, Thaw was judged sane and freed. *From the Bain News Service, Library of Congress.*

Thaw's siren, Evelyn Nesbit. She married Thaw in 1905 and testified in his defense at both trials amid rumors that Thaw's family paid her for her favorable comments. She divorced Thaw in 1915. Photograph by Gertrude Käsebier, circa 1900. *From the Library of Congress.*

peculiar eyes attracted much attention at his trial. Waite's eyes are smaller than those of Thaw."[222]

Others contemplated possible brain damage as the source of Waite's malignant motives and cited a peculiar discovery during the autopsy conducted after Waite's execution. The brain tissue showed signs that at some point during his youth, Arthur Warren Waite suffered from meningitis—an infection that can lead to a high fever. This finding was consistent with the symptoms of a childhood illness that Waite described to Dr. Karpas.

Something else Waite said during one of his sessions with Dr. Karpas also fueled speculation. Waite told Dr. Karpas that when he was in college, he fell down a staircase and "was out of his head."[223]

———⟫◦⟪———

Arthur Warren Waite continued to be the talk of New York for years after his execution. As late as 1952, the Coliseum elevator operator—a gregarious fellow named Tony—still told the story of the doctor who wasn't.[224]

———⟫◦⟪———

On June 8, 1918, Arthur's mother, Sarah J. Waite, died of hyperthyroidism and myocarditis just days before her sixty-first birthday. The attending physician didn't include a contributory factor on the death certificate, but the emotional strain of Arthur's trial and subsequent execution had caused her health to erode. She was buried in Fair Plains Cemetery in Grand Rapids next to her husband, Warren.

———⟫◦⟪———

Clara Louise Peck didn't spend the rest of her life pining over Arthur Warren Waite. On June 1, 1920, she wed her childhood sweetheart, John Caulfield, in Pasadena, California. She died in 1964 at the age of seventy-six.

———⟫◦⟪———

Percy Seaman Peck devoted countless hours to Liberty Loan fundraisers during the First World War. After suffering from a stroke, he died on September 13, 1944, at the age of sixty-five. He was interred at Woodlawn Cemetery in Grand Rapids, Michigan.

———⟫◦⟪———

Catherine Peck, who survived Waite's scheming, which included ground glass mixed in a jar of marmalade and probably typhus, diphtheria and who knows what other dangerous germs, died of natural causes in Grand Rapids on February 21, 1927, at the home of Percy Peck. She was eighty-one years old.

The Reverend Dr. Alfred Wesley Wishart continued to helm the Fountain Street Baptist Church. When the structure burned down in 1917, he spearheaded the campaign to build a new church, which opened in 1924. In 1928—three years after the Scopes Monkey Trial—Wishart staged a public debate with famed attorney Clarence Darrow.

Characterized by investigators and reporters alike as a Sherlock Holmes who played a major role in exposing Waite's crimes, Wishart died on April 25, 1933, at the age of sixty-seven. The *New York Times* wrote a glowing obituary for the Grand Rapids native. The article praised Wishart for his role in solving one of the city's most infamous cases but erred in the degree of his zealousness by stating that "he and Dr. Perry Schurtz, a physician, stole the [John Peck's] body from its grave."[225]

NOTES

INTRODUCTION

1 Direct examination of Arthur Warren Waite, *The People of the State of New York v. Arthur Warren Waite*, New York Supreme Court trial transcript, Trial #3241, May 22, 1916, Stenographer No. 2679, Reels 400–01, Crime in New York 1850–1950, Special Collections, Lloyd Sealy Library, John Jay College of Criminal Justice, City University of New York, 641–765. Hereafter, *People v. Waite.*

2. This version of John Peck's final moments was based on Waite's trial testimony. However, John Peck's cause of death was hotly debated in court. The state contended that Waite smothered his father-in-law with a pillow on top of a chloroform-soaked rag to prevent his moans from waking Clara, which Waite subsequently admitted, but Dr. Otto Schultze testified that Peck died from arsenic poisoning. Waite's statements in court clearly indicate his belief that he smothered John Peck, but it is possible Waite didn't apply enough pressure or apply pressure long enough to suffocate his victim, and instead John Peck died shortly after from the aftereffects of poison. It is also possible that, given Waite's defense strategy, he lied about smothering Peck in the first place.

Chapter 1

3. Warren and Jennie Waite also had a daughter, Edith. Born in 1875, Edith married Frank W. Davie in 1896.

4. Hannah Carpenter was John E. Peck's second wife. His first marriage, to a Newburg, New York wagon maker's daughter, ended in divorce.

5. Biographical sketch, *Grand Rapids Herald*, March 16, 1916. Also, *Grand Rapids and Kent County Michigan: Historical Account of Their Progress from First Settlement to the Present Time*, Vol. 2. Edited by Ernest B. Fisher (Chicago: Robert O. Law Company, 1918), 288–89.

6. Cross-examination of Clara Louise Peck, *People v. Waite*. Clara gave this account of her courtship with Waite during her trial testimony.

7. *Grand Rapids Herald*, March 25, 1916.

8. Ibid., March 24, 1916.

9. Percy passed the Michigan Bar in 1900 and graduated from the University of Michigan's school of pharmacy in 1903.

10. State of Michigan, Department of Public Health, Vital Records, Michigan Death Indexes 1867–1914. Return of the Deaths of the County of Kent for the Quarter Ending December 31, 1896, 55–56. Entry for "Bessie Peck," Record No. 5160, filed May 19, 1897. Microfilm Reel 5, Library of Michigan. Bessie Peck died on February 10, 1896, at age fifteen. Her death record gives "heart trouble" as the cause.

11. Percy gave a lengthy statement about the case in the *Grand Rapids News*, March 27, 1916.

12. Direct examination of Arthur Warren Waite, *People v. Waite*. It is possible that Arthur wanted to delay the wedding until he could acquire bacteria cultures to poison the Pecks. He later testified to beginning his study of bacteriology in August, but the evidence suggests that he didn't acquire most of the cultures until October.

13. Percy married Mary Ellen Ferris in 1902, but she was familiarly known as "Ella."

14. *Grand Rapids News*, September 10, 1915.

Chapter 2

15. The telegram was sent at 8:44 a.m. on Monday, March 13.

16. At the trial, "K. Adams" did not state why she chose this pseudonym, but she later commented to the press about having a recently married friend by that name.

17. *Grand Rapids Herald*, March 24, 1916. Evidently, "K. Adams" wanted Percy Peck to believe the message emanated from a resident of the Coliseum. It is possible that the sender dictated the message to the clerk as a further way of ensuring her anonymity. Based on the loose scrawl of the handwriting on the original document, Wishart and later Swann both believed an elderly man wrote the message, and according to news reports, Western Union records indicated that a man filed the message for sending, which led to all sorts of speculation. According to testimony at the trial, a woman did in fact send the message but was most likely prompted by an elderly relative.

18. Direct examination of Dr. Perry Schurtz, *People v. Waite*. Dr. Schurtz described the autopsy during his testimony.

19. Direct examination of Joseph Sprattler, *People v. Waite*.

20. *Sun* (New York), May 24, 1916. The subsequent news coverage of the case contains several versions of this statement. While the wording varies slightly, the meaning is consistent. Waite wanted to block the autopsy on John Peck's remains.

21. *New York Tribune*, March 24, 1916.

22. According to several news accounts, a team of guards stood watch over the grave to ensure that no one would steal John Peck's body. Apparently, they suspected that Waite would attempt to break open the vault and either destroy or dispose of the remains.

23. *Grand Rapids Press*, March 24, 1916.

Chapter 3

24. The March 25, 1916 *Grand Rapids Press* contained an interview with Wishart, who detailed his New York investigation.

25. Even after Dr. Vaughn discovered arsenic in John Peck's stomach, both Drs. Moore and Porter made public statements standing by their diagnoses. Portions of their statements appeared in the March 23, 1916 edition of the *Grand Rapids Herald*. Dr. Moore was the physician on call for the Park Avenue Hotel, where Catherine Peck lived. He entered the case when she asked him to look after her brother.

26. *Sun* (New York), March 24, 1916; *Grand Rapids Herald*, March 25, 1916.

27. *Grand Rapids Herald*, March 13, 1916.

28. These quotes attributed to Waite were repeated by Percy and Ella Peck to a *Grand Rapids Herald* reporter from memory and subsequently appeared in the March 25, 1916 edition.

29. *Sun* (New York), March 28, 1916. Clara recalled this statement to Mancuso when he interviewed her in Grand Rapids. Mancuso subsequently rehashed it in a public statement.

30. *Directory of Directors in the City of New York* (New York: Directory of Directors Company, 1915). In 1916, the Schindler National Detective Agency was one of the best-known and most prestigious groups of private investigators in the United States. The organization was run by Raymond C. Schindler, president, treasurer and director; Walter S. Schindler, secretary, manager and director; and John F. Schindler, vice-president and treasurer. Their offices were located at 149 Broadway.

31. *Grand Rapids Press*, March 25, 1916. Accounts conflict about when Swann first became involved in the case. According to Rupert Hughes's biography of Raymond Schindler, Swann was reluctant and didn't believe the evidence gathered by this point was sufficient to warrant an investigation of Waite. Wishart, however, told the *Grand Rapids Press* that Swann became involved on Friday, March 17. Contemporary news accounts also suggest Swann opened an official line of inquiry at about the time Waite returned from Grand Rapids.

32. Raymond C. Schindler, "The Bogus Doctor Who Wanted to Be Rich," *Buffalo Sunday Courier Magazine*, July 9, 1922, 6. Schindler was the only one involved with the case to write about it. His one-page article presents an interesting account of the early investigation.

CHAPTER 4

33. Schindler's account conflicts with contemporary newspaper stories about this initial search of the Coliseum apartment. Most newspaper accounts have Swann's men conducting an official search, while Schindler's suggests an unofficial sweep.

34. *New York Herald*, March 26, 1916. Waite called the apartment of Dorothy Von Palmenberg.

35. Direct testimony of Arthur Swinton, *People v. Waite*. This was the day that Arthur Swinton ran into Waite and his "nurse" in the restaurant of the Plaza Hotel.

36. *Grand Rapids Herald*, March 25, 1916.

37. On January 1, 1907, the New York State Health Department banned the use of arsenic, as well as other poisonous alkaloids, in embalming. The ban stemmed from a criminal case in which the defendant, Albert T. Patrick, accused of poisoning William Marsh Rice, tried to deflect

blame by contending the arsenic found in Rice's remains resulted from embalming, not murder. By the time of the Waite trial, Michigan had also banned the use of arsenic in embalming.

38. *New York Tribune*, March 29, 1916. Cimiotti gave this account to Swann.

39. *New York World*, March 25, 1916. A few days later, Catherine Peck issued a statement rejecting the possibility of suicide.

40. *New York Tribune*, March 23, 1916.

41. Ibid., March 24, 1916. This assertion caused reporters to compare the Peck case with the Maybrick case.

42. Direct examination of Arthur Warren Waite, *People v. Waite*.

43. Margaret contradicted herself on this point. She told reporters that Waite responded, "You know I didn't." She later testified that he admitted it.

44. *New York Herald*, March 26, 1916. Margaret Horton later claimed that she didn't know Waite signed them into the guest registry as "Dr. and Mrs. A.W. Walters," but this note suggests otherwise.

45. *Sun* (New York), May 23, 1916.

CHAPTER 5

46. The five men stayed in room 431 under the names of F.X. Mancuso (not fictitious), H.A. Barnard, A.N. Hubbard, J.A. Brown and Guy T. Gibbons (who stayed in a separate room).

47. *Grand Rapids Herald*, March 24, 1916.

48. Ibid., March 25, 1916.

49. *Sun* (New York), March 28, 1916. Mancuso gave a lengthy statement to the press, in which he detailed the discoveries he made in Grand Rapids. Mancuso suggests that Waite went trawling for victims when he returned to the United States, but the letters Waite and Clara exchanged while Waite worked in Africa suggest that he may have targeted her family before he returned to Michigan.

50. *New York Tribune*, March 29, 1916.

51. Percy discussed this suspicion in his statement published in the *Grand Rapids News*, March 27, 1916.

52. The statement of the anonymous friend is quoted in the March 29 edition of the *Grand Rapids Herald*.

53. *Grand Rapids Herald*, March 23, 1916.

54. Ibid.

55. Ibid.

56. Clara was twenty-seven in March 1916.
57. Marie Dille, "Mrs. Waite Made Will Recently in Husband's Favor, Says Relative," *Grand Rapids Herald*, March 23, 1916.
58. *Grand Rapids Herald*, March 24, 1916. Hillier testified at the Grand Jury Hearing, but her testimony is not part of the extant record. She also did not testify at Waite's trial. In the portion of the trial transcript devoted to jury selection, there is a reference to the possibility that she might testify, but for unknown reasons, she never appeared as a witness.
59. *Grand Rapids Herald*, March 24 and March 26, 1916; *Sun* (New York), March 25, 1916; *New York Tribune*, March 24, 1916.
60. *Grand Rapids Herald*, March 24, 1916.
61. Waite played on courts around New York with his friend, Cornell tennis star Abraham Bassford. Waite, who was known as a crafty player who excelled at net shots, won the Metropolitan Indoor Championship in February 1916 when he defeated Bassford.
62. *Grand Rapids Herald*, March 24, 1916.
63. This portion of Mancuso's statement is from the *Grand Rapids Herald*, March 25, 1916.
64. *Grand Rapids Herald*, March 24, 1916. Curiously, Schindler does not give much credit to either Dr. Wishart or Dr. Schurtz. Schindler, according to some sources, tended to play up his role in investigations, so it is best to keep this in mind when considering his account of the Peck case.

CHAPTER 6

65. *Grand Rapids Herald*, March 24, 1916.
66. Ibid., March 25, 1916, contains the wording of the note in its entirety. The note contradicts many published accounts that, upon reading about Margaret Horton, Clara's faith in her husband began to crumble. The Waites left Grand Rapids Friday morning. While en route, Arthur made his confession to Swann. Thus, it is more likely that Clara lost faith after reading news accounts of Arthur's confession.
67. *Evening World* (New York), March 25, 1916.
68. *Grand Rapids Herald*, March 25, 1916. She gave Waite money to invest in three installments: $5,000 on October 1, 1915; $30,000 on December 15, 1915; and $6,000 on January 17, 1916.
69. *Grand Rapids Herald*, March 26, 1916. The press characterized the nature of these relationships as "wholly social." According to some accounts, the

box contained Waite's diary, although it is more likely they found a "little black book" of names and addresses.

70. Swann did not disclose specifics about these papers, only that they pertained to the acquisition of poisons. This secrecy led the press to conclude that the papers contained receipts for arsenic. In fact, this cache included letters, purporting to come from legitimate doctors, which Waite fraudulently used to acquire bacteria at laboratories throughout the city. The papers may also have included prescriptions for drugs containing poisons.

71. Swann kept Timmerman's identity from the press until the grand jury hearing.

72. *Sun* (New York), May 24, 1916.

73. *New York Herald*, March 25, 1916; *Sun* (New York), March 25, 1916.

74. *Sun* (New York), March 25, 1916.

75. *New York Herald*, March 25, 1916. Waite's lack of emotion struck Swann as so odd that he wondered if he was a drug addict. Swann later told a reporter, "I asked him [Waite] if he was a habitual user of narcotics or similar drugs. He replied that he had never taken a sleeping potion in his life until Wednesday, that he never had needed any."

76. This exchange was quoted in the (New York) *World*, March 25, 1916, and repeated in the *Grand Rapids Herald*, March 25, 1916; a very similar exchange appears in the *New York Herald*'s front-page story from March 25, 1916.

77. The *Evening World* (New York) edition of March 23, 1916, describes Swann's suspicious about this as-yet-unknown woman known only as "Mrs. A.W. Walters."

78. *Evening World* (New York), March 25, 1916.

79. Margaret Horton's full statement can be found in the *Grand Rapids Herald*, March 25, 1916; the *Evening World* (New York), March 25, 1916; and the *Sun* (New York), March 25, 1916.

80. *Grand Rapids Herald*, March 25, 1916.

81. At first, Waite was placed in Ward 44—Bellevue's prison ward—but shortly thereafter moved to a more spacious room in the alcoholics' ward. This would be necessary to accommodate the many investigators who would later question him.

CHAPTER 7

82. Marie Dille, "These Hypnotic Eyes Caused a Fluttering in Feminine Hearts and Aided Handsome Young Dentist to Climb Society Ladder," *Grand Rapids Herald*, March 25, 1916.

83. *Grand Rapids Herald*, March 25, 1916.

84. *New York Times*, March 25, 1916. "The shock has had a serious effect upon her," wrote a *New York Times* correspondent, "and her condition is said to be much worse."

85. Clara's statement indicts the press for fabricating quotations. She may be referring to the message she allegedly gave to Waite's parents when they traveled to New York just a day earlier. If she did ask them to send such a message, she likely expected the message to remain private. As news about the case evolved, she may have felt like her affirmation of undying love made her look like a fool, so she may have attempted to discredit the message at this point.

86. *Grand Rapids Herald*, March 26, 1916.

87. *New York Evening World*, March 28, 1916; *New York Tribune*, March 29, 1916. Some news accounts state that Swann interviewed tennis friends of Waite's who became mysteriously ill, suggesting that Waite used them as guinea pigs. Swann, however, denounced this as an utter falsehood to a *New York Tribune* writer.

88. *Sun* (New York), March 28, 1916. According to Schindler, Margaret Horton was never a suspect, but contemporary news reports indicate otherwise. An item in the *Grand Rapids Press*, April 5, 1916, under the headline "Mrs. Horton Is Eliminated as Suspect," states that after a thorough investigation of Margaret Horton's movements, Swann was convinced she played no part in Waite's plot.

89. *Grand Rapids Herald*, March 28, 1916.

90. According to some reports, Swann met with Margaret Horton as early as Thursday, but in response to a reporter, Swann emphatically denied that he or any of his agents had met with her until Saturday. He said that the first time he heard the name "Margaret Horton" was when a *World* reporter phoned him and told him that he had just interviewed "Mrs. A.W. Walters." At the time, he said, he didn't feel as if "Mrs. A.W. Walters" was a person of interest.

91. Harry Mack Horton was not present when Dooling questioned Margaret about her relationship with Arthur, but he was present during Margaret's interviews with the press. This may explain the lie she told reporters.

92. *Grand Rapids Herald*, March 27, 1916; *New York Herald*, March 28, 1916.
93. *New York Tribune*, March 29, 1916.
94. *Grand Rapids Herald*, March 29, 1916.
95. *New York Tribune*, March 29, 1916.
96. *Grand Rapids News*, March 27, 1916.
97. Ibid., March 30, 1916.
98. *Grand Rapids Herald*, March 26, 1916; *Grand Rapids News*, March 26, 1916.
99. *Richmond Times-Dispatch*, April 16, 1916.
100. *Grand Rapids Herald*, March 26, 1916.

CHAPTER 8

101. News accounts vary on this aspect of the case. Some stories have Waite making two separate confessions, first to Frank and later to Frank and Raymond Schindler.
102. *Grand Rapids Herald*, March 29, 1916. Percy Peck told the press that Catherine Peck requested Deuel handle Waite's case. The Peck family later issued a public statement in which they denied making any such request.
103. Grand Rapids articles often compared Waite to Jekyll and Hyde. It is possible that Waite, aware of this comparison, conjured up a new version of the famous tale with the hope he could pin some of the blame on his evil other self. It is also possible, given the similarities in their stories, that Waite borrowed a stratagem attempted by slayer George W. Wood.
104. The *Grand Rapids Herald*, in a sidebar published in the March 28, 1916 edition, placed the remarkably similar statements of Wood and Waite side by side.
105. *Grand Rapids Herald*, March 29, 1916. Schindler recalled this bit of the interview.
106. *Grand Rapids Herald*, March 30, 1916. This exchange attributed to Potter, Kane and Waite was recollected by Swann in an exclusive interview with a *Grand Rapids Herald* reporter.
107. *Grand Rapids Herald*, March 29, 1916.
108. *New York Tribune*, March 29, 1916.
109. *Grand Rapids Herald*, March 30, 1916.
110. *New York Tribune*, March 29, 1916.
111. Her subsequent testimony and dogged loyalty to Waite also suggests the falsity of this accusation.
112. The entire statement appears in the *New York Times*, March 30, 1916.

CHAPTER 9

113. *Evening Telegram* (New York), May 23, 1916.

114. Doyle, "The Boscombe Valley Mystery."

115. *New York Herald*, April 1, 1916.

116. *The People of the State of New York v. Arthur Warren Waite*, Cal. No. 19307, No. 109983, filed March 31, 1916. New York City Municipal Archives.

117. *New York Times*, April 1, 1916; *New York Herald*, April 1, 1916.

118. *Grand Rapids Herald*, March 30, 1916.

119. Margaret Horton's note is undated but was published in several newspapers, including the March 30, 1916 edition of the *Daybook* (Chicago). The actual note is located in the New York *World Telegram* and *Sun* biography file for "Margaret Horton" in the Library of Congress.

120. According to some news reports, Arthur's letters to Margaret wound up on Swann's desk. Some reports indicate that Margaret betrayed Arthur by giving the letters to Swann. Her testimony at the trial, however, proves that she did neither.

121. *Sun* (New York), April 2, 1916. News of the confession appeared across the nation on Monday, April 3. The *Grand Rapids News*, April 3, 1916, ran a page-one item under the headline "WAITE UNABLE TO LEAVE BED."

CHAPTER 10

122. *Sun* (New York), March 28, 1916.

123. *Evening World* (New York), April 4, 1916; *Grand Rapids Press*, April 4, 1916.

124. *New York Times*, March 26, 1916.

125. A lengthy transcript of the interview appears in the April 6, 1916 edition of the *New York Tribune*.

126. *Grand Rapids Press*, April 17, 1916.

127. *New York Tribune*, April 18, 1916.

128. Because Waite's defense relied on the idea that only an insane person would commit such depraved acts, it is possible that Waite exaggerated the extent of his attempts to murder the Pecks. Clara's statements to Mancuso at this point, however, prove some of Waite's testimony at the subsequent trial.

129. *New York Tribune*, April 19, 1916; *Sun* (New York), April 21, 1916. According to an item in the *Grand Rapids Press*, April 7, 1916, Waite

"inoculated himself with the germs of virulent typhoid in order to note on himself their effects." Waite apparently became so sick he had to call for a doctor. This raises a few possibilities to explain the presence of typhoid in Clara's blood: Waite may have also experimented on Clara, or Clara may have become sick when she caught it from her husband.

130. Mancuso did not reveal the names, and none of the news reports reveal the identities of Waite's many lady friends. *Sun* (New York), April 21, 1916.

131. *New York Dramatic Mirror*, May 6, 1918.

132. *New York Herald*, May 18, 1916.

CHAPTER 11

133. The official transcript of testimony is located in the collections of the Lloyd Sealy Library at the John Jay Library of Criminal Justice, which archives cases from the era. In addition, several New York newspapers sent reporters to cover the trial. The *Evening Telegram* (New York) coverage tends to consolidate several answers into single responses, while the *Sun* (New York) and the *New York Herald* articles provide a better sense of the actual back-and-forth between lawyers and their witnesses and include other aspects of the trial atmosphere—such as an instance when a juror laughed—that are not part of the official record.

134. *New York Herald*, May 23, 1916.

135. Examination of Talesmen, *People v. Waite*; *Evening Telegram* (New York), May 22, 1916; *New York Herald*, May 23, 1916.

136. Fifty-six potential jurors, or talesmen, were questioned during jury selection.

137. *Evening Telegram* (New York), May 22, 1916; *Evening Post* (New York); *New York Herald*, May 23, 1916; *New York Sun*, May 23, 1916. The jury selected consisted of the following: Robert Neill, mechanical engineer; Peter Hebel, merchant; Thaddeus S. Barlow, superintendent; Paul D. Case, assistant secretary; George A. Helme, "capitalist"; James H. Betts, insurance agent; Edwin M. Friedlander, broker; Thomas Widdercombe, accountant; James N. Jeffares, manager; Stephen A. Douglass, electrical engineer; Hugh F. Donnelly, real estate agent; Joseph H. Trant, writer.

138. At the time of the trial, Frank Waite was a resident of New York, residing at 3210 Hull Avenue in the Bronx.

139. *New York Herald*, May 23, 1916.

140. *Evening Telegram* (New York), May 22, 1916, "10 P.M. Extra."

141. Opening of Judge Edward Swann, *People v. Waite.*
142. Direct examination of Dr. Albertus Adair Moore, *People v. Waite.* Diarrhea is a symptom of typhoid fever, but when Brothers later began to question Moore about this, Deuel objected, and Shearn sustained the objection.
143. *New York Herald,* May 23, 1916.
144. Direct examination of Dr. Albertus Adair Moore, *People v. Waite.*
145. *New York Sun,* May 23, 1916.
146. *New York Tribune,* May 23, 1916.
147. Ibid.
148. (New York) *Evening Telegram,* May 23, 1916.
149. Direct examination of Dr. Victor C. Vaughn, *People v. Waite.* The provenance of this fluid became a point of contention during the trial.
150. Direct examination of Dr. Otto Schultze, *People v. Waite.*
151. Direct examination of Dr. Richard W. Muller, *People v. Waite.*
152. Direct examination of Dr. Richard H. Timmerman, *People v. Waite.*
153. (New York) *Evening Telegram,* May 23, 1916.
154. Direct examination of Arthur Swinton, *People v. Waite.*
155. *New York Tribune,* May 24, 1916.
156. Direct examination of Eugene Oliver Kane, *People v. Waite.*
157. Cross-examination of Eugene Oliver Kane, *People v. Waite.* See the March 31, 1916 *New York Times* for a discussion of Kane's shady background.

Chapter 12

158. *Sun* (New York), May 25, 1916.
159. Direct examination of Elizabeth B. Hardwicke, *People v. Waite.* Hardwicke was not asked why she chose the "K. Adams" pseudonym. The identity of the person she said asked her to send the telegram also remains a minor mystery in the case, although at the time, several people suspected Dr. Cornell.
160. Direct examination of Clara Louise Peck, *People v. Waite.*
161. Direct examination of Clara Louise Peck, resumed, *People v. Waite.*
162. *New York Herald,* May 25, 1916.
163. Cross-examination of Clara Louise Peck, *People v. Waite.*
164. *New York Herald,* May 25, 1916.
165. *Evening Telegram* (New York), May 24, 1916.
166. *Sun* (New York), May 25, 1916. Portions of Margaret Horton's testimony appeared in several New York dailies, but the content and tone

of the coverage vary widely. A reluctant witness, Margaret Horton was obstinate, even hostile during Brothers's examination—an attitude best captured by the *New York Sun*'s correspondent.

167. In March, Margaret Horton recounted this conversation for reporters, but in this earlier version, she said Waite denied the accusation. In some newspaper accounts, this exchange is presented as quite hostile. Margaret, at first, doesn't answer the question, prompting Brothers to ask again.

168. Direct examination of Margaret Weaver Horton, *People v. Waite*.

169. Cross-examination of Margaret Weaver Horton, *People v. Waite*.

170. *Sun* (New York), May 25, 1916.

CHAPTER 13

171. At the time, flypaper contained arsenic. In the infamous Maybrick murder trial of 1889, Florence Maybrick, accused of poisoning her husband, testified that she obtained arsenic by soaking flypaper in water, although she claimed she wanted the poison for cosmetic use. She was convicted and sentenced to death but was released in 1904 and became a sensation on the lecture tour. It is probable that Waite knew about the Maybrick case, which made headlines across the United States.

172. *Sun* (New York), May 26, 1916.

173. *New York Herald*, May 26, 1916.

174. Direct examination of Arthur Warren Waite, *People v. Waite*.

175. Cross-examination of Arthur Warren Waite, *People v. Waite*.

176. Ibid.

177. Direct examination of Catherine A. Peck, *People v. Waite*.

178. It is unclear when Waite began to plot the downfall of the Peck family. Waite testified to plotting the murders as early as 1914, when he returned from South Africa. Dr. Karpas's testimony indicates he planned the murders in the interval between his engagement and his nuptials on September 9, 1915. If Waite told Dr. Karpas the truth about his plot, then he planned to kill Clara all along and most likely would have made an attempt when she returned to New York. In an article in the British pulp the *Thriller*, Phyllis Lewis states that Waite had already begun his attempt on Clara's life, and a blood test, taken after Waite's arrest, revealed the presence of typhus. This timeline, and Waite's testimony, also suggests that his attempts to murder Catherine Peck may have served a secondary

purpose; he likely used her to experiment with various substances before he set his grand scheme in motion.

179. Direct examination of Dr. Morris J. Karpas, *People v. Waite*.
180. Ibid.
181. Cross-examination of Dr. Morris J. Karpas, *People v. Waite*.
182. Direct examination of Dr. Alan Ross Dieffendorf, *People v. Waite*.

Chapter 14

183. Direct examination of Dr. Ely Smith Jelliffe, *People v. Waite*.
184. Closing argument of Walter Rogers Deuel, *People v. Waite*.
185. Closing argument of George Brothers, *People v. Waite*.
186. Justice Shearn's instructions to the jury, *People v. Waite*.
187. *Evening Telegram* (New York), May 27, 1916.
188. *New York Herald*, May 28, 1916. Newspapers compared Waite's trial to those of six other infamous criminals: Harry K. Thaw (nineteen days), Roland Burnham Molineux (twenty-one days), Carlyle Harris (fourteen days), Albert T. Patrick (forty-six days), Robert Buchanan (thirty-seven days) and Charles Becker (first trial, sixteen days; second trial, fourteen days).
189. Robert Rohde, "Peddling Poems from the Death House," *New York Tribune*, June 11, 1916.
190. *Evening Telegram* (New York), May 27, 1916; *Sun* (New York), May 28, 1916.
191. *New York Tribune*, May 28, 1916.
192. *Sun* (New York), May 28, 1916.
193. *Evening Telegram* (New York), May 27, 1916.
194. *New York Herald*, May 28, 1916.
195. *New York Tribune*, May 28, 1916.
196. Ibid.
197. Ibid.
198. These precautions led to a false rumor that Waite had attempted to kill himself on the morning of May 28.
199. *Evening Telegram* (New York), May 29, 1916.
200. Ibid., May 28, 1916.
201. Sentencing, *People v. Waite*.

CHAPTER 15

202. Rohde, "Peddling Poems from the Death House."

203. *Evening Telegram* (New York), June 1, 1916.

204. Ibid.

205. *Daybook* (Chicago), June 3, 1916.

206. *Sun* (New York), June 12, 1916; Phyllis Lewis, "The Case of Arthur Warren Waite, the Death Dealing Doctor, Pt. 2." *Thriller* vol. 1, no. 45 (December 14, 1929), 1142–44. The disposition of Arthur's jailhouse poetry remains unknown. A few appeared in the *Sun* (June 12, 1916) and the *New York Times* (June 11, 1916). One piece did appear in a 1929 feature about the case in the British tabloid the *Thriller*.

207. Rohde, "Peddling Poems from the Death House."

208. *New York Times*, July 26, 1916. On July 25, 1916, Waite cut himself, prompting yet another wave of suicide rumors. Osborne subsequently addressed the press: "The scratch is infinitesimal. It was not even serious enough for hospital treatment. Waite is passionately fond of attracting attention to himself, and this, I believe, was the motive for his act."

209. *Daily Standard Union* (Brooklyn, NY), October 17, 1916.

210. State of Michigan Department of State, County of Kent, Certificate of Death for Warren Winfield Waite, March 23, 1917, No. 501.

211. *New York Times*, May 24, 1917.

212. A good eyewitness account of Becker's execution can be found in the July 30, 1915 *New York Times*.

CHAPTER 16

213. *Syracuse Daily Journal*, May 24, 1917.

214. Ibid.

215. Ibid.

216. Ibid., May 25, 1917. The prison chaplain, Dr. A.N. Peterson, was present during this exchange and later recounted the conversation for reporters.

217. *Evening Telegram* (New York), May 25, 1917. News accounts differ slightly regarding this exchange, but the gist of Waite's statement is consistent. Also see the *Sun* (New York), May 25, 1917.

218. *New York Times*, May 24, 1917.

219. *Syracuse Daily Journal*, May 25, 1917.

220. *New York Times*, May 24, 1917.
221. *Syracuse Daily Journal*, May 24, 1917.
222. *Day Book* (Chicago), May 29, 1916, noon edition.
223. Direct examination of Dr. Morris J. Karpas, *People v. Waite.*
224. Lawrence G. Blochman, "Murder on Riverside Drive: The True Mystery I Wish I'd Created." Blochman's article appeared in many newspapers, including the *Milwaukee Sentinel*, June 8, 1952.
225. *New York Times*, April 25, 1933.

BIBLIOGRAPHY

DOCUMENTS

The People of the State of New York vs. Arthur Warren Waite. Calendar Number 19307, Indictment Number 109983, filed March 31, 1916. New York City Municipal Archives.

The People of the State of New York vs. Arthur Warren Waite. New York Supreme Court trial transcript, Trial #3241, May 22, 1916, Stenographer No. 2679, Reels 400–01, Crime in New York 1850–1950, Special Collections, Lloyd Sealy Library, John Jay College of Criminal Justice, The City University of New York.

Sing Sing Correctional Facility Records Group B0147. Admission registers for prisoners to be executed, 1891–1946, entry for Arthur Warren Waite, prisoner No. 67281, New York State Archives, Albany, New York.

Sing Sing Correctional Facility Records Group B1244. Log of actions relating to inmates scheduled for execution, 1915–1967, entry for Arthur Warren Waite, prisoner No. 67281, New York State Archives, Albany, New York.

NEWSPAPERS

Daily Standard Union (Brooklyn, NY)

Day Book (Chicago)

Evening Telegram (New York)

Evening World (New York)

Grand Rapids Herald

Grand Rapids News

Grand Rapids Press

Kingston (New York) *Daily Freeman*

Milwaukee Sentinel

New York Dramatic Mirror

New York Herald

New York Times

New York Tribune

Sun (New York)

Syracuse (New York) *Daily Journal*

BOOKS AND MAGAZINES

Directory of Directors in the City of New York. New York: Directory of Directors Company, 1915.

Doyle, Arthur Conan. "The Boscombe Valley Mystery." *The Adventures of Sherlock Holmes.* New York: Harper & Brothers, 1892.

Hughes, Rupert. *The Complete Detective: Being the Life and Strange and Exciting Cases of Raymond Schindler, Master Detective.* New York: Sheridan House, 1950.

Lewis, Phyllis. "The Case of Arthur Warren Waite, the Death Dealing Doctor, Pt. 1." Pts. 1–4, *Thriller* 1, no. 42 (November 23, 1929): 1069–72; no. 43 (November 30, 1929): 1094–96; no. 44 (December 7, 1929): 1117–20; no. 45 (December 14, 1929): 1142–44.

Silbar, Howard. "Michigan's Poisoning Maniac." *Detective Files* (March 1978): 22–25, 43–45.

INDEX

ABOUT THE AUTHOR

Tobin T. Buhk is a freelance author specializing in true crime. To research his first book, *Cause of Death* (Prometheus Books, 2007), he volunteered in a county morgue, watching as his co-author, Kent County chief medical examiner Dr. Stephen D. Cohle, unraveled puzzling forensic mysteries. A second collaboration with Dr. Cohle resulted in *Skeletons in the Closet* (Prometheus, 2008). Buhk's love of history and fascination with true crime led to *True Crime Michigan* (Stackpole Books, 2011), *True Crime in the Civil War* (Stackpole, 2012), *The Shocking Case of Helmuth Schmidt* (The History Press, 2013) and *Michigan's Strychnine Saint* (The History Press, 2014).